Small Group
Outreach

Turning Groups
Inside Out

Jeffrey Arnold

InterVarsity Press
Downers Grove, Illinois

InterVarsity Press
P.O. Box 1400, Downers Grove, IL 60515
World Wide Web: www.ivpress.com
E-mail: mail@ivpress.com

InterVarsity Press® is the book-publishing division of InterVarsity Christian Fellowship/USA®, a student movement active on campus at hundreds of universities, colleges and schools of nursing in the United States of America, and a member movement of the International Fellowship of Evangelical Students. For information about local and regional activities, write Public Relations Dept., InterVarsity Christian Fellowship/USA, 6400 Schroeder Rd., P.O. Box 7895, Madison, WI 53707-7895.

Cover photograph: COMSTOCK, Inc.

ISBN 0-8308-1170-2

Printed in the United States of America ♾

Library of Congress Cataloging-in-Publication Data

Arnold, Jeffrey.
   Small group outreach : turning groups inside out / Jeffrey Arnold.
     p. cm.
   Includes bibliographical references.
   ISBN 0-8308-1170-2 (pbk. : alk. paper)
   1. Church group work. I. Title.
 BV652.2.A766   1998
 253'.7—dc21
                                                     98-18567
                                                        CIP

20 19 18 17 16 15 14 13 12 11 10 9 8 7 6 5 4 3 2 1

15 14 13 12 11 10 09 08 07 06 05 04 03 02 01 00 99 98

Introduction

Small groups need to be turned inside out.

Like Betsy's group, which invited non-Christians to take part in a study about Jesus. Or Alan's group, which carried groceries and touched lives on senior citizen shopping day at the local market. Or Kyle's college fellowship group, which volunteered weekly at an inner-city community center.

These groups, and others like them, are true communities of faith. We're not talking about the kind of community you live in. Nor do we mean the community that spends time together at your church or even in your small groups.

We are talking about the kind of community that transforms lives. A welcoming community that loves you. An accountable community that challenges you. A worshiping community that invites you into God's presence, and God into yours. A studying community that approaches Scripture with humility and a willingness to risk. A praying community that ministers God's love and intercedes on your behalf.

And an outreaching community that willingly shares what it has with others.

Heeding the Call

There is no shortage of helpful small group resources. The Christian small group movement has produced a plethora of books that examine the dynamics, strategies and practical needs of small groups.

Few books, however, specifically consider a group's outward focus. Groups attempting to reach beyond themselves to embrace their God-given mission to the world have had limited resources from which to choose.

Until now. This book uses a dynamic, time-oriented approach to move small groups toward outreach. Its overarching purpose is to foster within small groups a passion for ministry in a variety of forms—evangelism, service, mission and much more.

Using This Resource

Groups and individuals will find in this resource a large number of outreach ideas that span a broad spectrum of possibilities. The ideas include issues related to a group's focus on its own health, its support of a sponsoring congregation and its outreach to friends, neighbors, relatives, community and the world.

Your group cannot possibly do everything, and certainly not all at once. So how can it best utilize the ideas in this book for the purpose of doing outreach in a systematic manner? Here are three options:

Option 1: The potpourri method. Groups using this method begin by testing the ideas that they find most appealing. For example, a group may be intrigued by the book's discussion of the empty chair and sharing in groups of four. In regard to outreach, the group may embrace the ideas of an open/closed group and service evangelism. Members may go on to employ other outreach ideas as those ideas gain momentum in group discussion.

Option 2: The building block method. The building block method is a more systematic approach to outreach, and it is encouraged by the layout of this book. Under this system a group starts with basic outreach ideas and builds on them as time goes by. Perhaps a group creates a plan that intends

to use the empty chair and to share in groups of four (step 1)

for the leader to begin apprenticing and for the group to hold its first service outreach project (step 2)

for the group to invite newcomers and to study an introduction to the Christian faith together (step 3)

for the group to begin correspondence with a missionary, supporting him with prayer and kindness (step 4)

for the group to multiply, forming two groups (step 5)

You can begin by brainstorming outreach ideas for your group. Discard those that lack support. Lay out the rest in a step-by-step process that moves from simple to complex. Write the steps as group goals so that you can measure your progress.

Option 3: The life cycle method. This plan is similar to the building block method in that it takes a dynamic, time-oriented approach to the possibilities of group outreach. It differs in that it includes an understanding that most groups, meeting weekly, follow a natural life pattern during the course of a year. Therefore, certain outreach methods are deemed appropriate to certain time periods in a group's life cycle. You can learn more about this understanding of group life by attending a Pilgrimage Training Group seminar (based in Littleton, Colorado).

Here is what an outreach plan that follows a life cycle approach might look like:

Stage 1: Build community (6 to 12 weeks). As the group begins meeting in the fall, its primary concern is bonding and becoming a community. The outreach methods most helpful at this time are to use groups of four for ͜haring and to pray for the empty chair.

Stage 2: Learn and grow (6 to 12 weeks). This would be a great time to adopt a mission family and/or participate in a first service outreach project.

Stage 3: Develop ministry skills (6 to 12 weeks). The focus of the group begins to change and turn outward, so preparation may begin for an eventual group split (apprenticing, goal setting). This is also a great time to zero in on being an inviting group or to plan a short-term mission project.

Stage 4: Multiply ministry (6 to 12 weeks). During this time most groups birth other groups or participate in short-term projects or become an evangelistic Bible study. It is also a great time for the church to hold leadership training for those apprentices who find themselves in positions of leadership.

Who May Use This Resource

This resource is for those who want to explore the various dimensions and options of small group outreach. It is appropriate for individuals who are simply looking for new ideas. It is helpful for small group committees and task forces in congregations and campus ministries. It can be used in the ongoing training of small group leaders or as a leadership resource for a small group library. Pastors and church leaders may find ideas to energize the different small groups that exist in their congregations. Sunday school classes may study this book, as well as women's circles, evangelism committees and local ecumenical gatherings.

But the greatest benefit of this book will be to small groups. A small group may use this resource by purchasing one book for every person (or couple). Individuals may read the chapter and then turn to the "Reflection on the Chapter" questions found in the appendix under each appropriate chapter heading. When the group meets, it may use the "Small Group Discussion" questions that are provided in the appendix.

No group will be able to implement all of the ideas in this book. They are presented in a format that allows you to view each option and then interact with it in individual and group reflection. As your group members consider the choices they can make, God may begin calling you to a specific kind of ministry.

The appendix contains questions and small group experiences for each chapter so that individuals and groups using this resource may have guided opportunities to interact. There is also a brief resource section at the end of each chapter for groups and/or individuals desiring study deeper of a particular topic.

Finding the Harvest
"The harvest is plentiful."

Jesus made this statement, in John 4, to his disciples, who had just gone into town to pick up food. Unbeknownst to them, the town was following them out to meet Jesus. But they were preoccupied with their lunches, worrying over who had the burger without onions and why they had small fries when they ordered large fries.

We can be like those disciples. Small groups are great at providing care and support. They are not always great at including outsiders in God's blessings. Perhaps this is true because we are busy or because we are always facing difficult situations in our groups. Perhaps we are already serving in our churches and just want to be with people who are like us. Perhaps we are insecure and want to feel ministered to, without having to care about others.

The challenge for groups and individuals using this resource is to prepare to move from self to other, from one small group to many small groups, from a static ministry (my group) to a dynamic ministry (God's groups) and from inreach to outreach.

This resource is intended to help groups that have never performed dynamic ministry to grow—so that people who don't know Jesus may come.

1

Becoming a SAFE Group

The conversation around the coffee machine at the plant was more animated than usual. The week before, an employee had been struck by a crane and killed. The plant shut down for a few days, and a memorial service was held for the accident victim.

Today the talk was about the memorial service. Some found that it was unlike any funeral they had ever attended. For one thing, the service was not dreary. It actually seemed upbeat in a reverent kind of way. There was talk of heaven and Jesus and victory over sin and death. For another thing, the family of their coworker had been surrounded by loving hands and caring friends from the moment the accident happened. The man had been a Christian, quiet and hard working. Now his peers saw the spiritual and emotional support that had been behind him—it still existed for his family. They did not miss its significance.

Lingering over their coffee break at work, several individuals expressed an almost wistful desire to have what their friend had. Somehow they sensed hope and victory in the midst of death and defeat.

Few of the workers were aware that their friend's life was enhanced by a small group that knew how to care. When a crisis situation presented itself, the group immediately mobilized to provide loving support. Their action made a powerful witness as the man's coworkers saw the church in action during a moment of vulnerability.

The Nature of Witness

We Christians are "walking billboards" for our faith. Everything from our choice of words to the way we work is a testimony either to the Lord who changes lives or to our unwillingness to let God work in us.

Christian leaders and authors have come to recognize this fact. Evangelism materials have evolved from focusing on what we do to looking at who we are. We now use words like *lifestyle, winsome, engaging, consistent* and *modeling* when we talk about witnessing. We realize that what matters most in evangelism is the level of love operating in and through God's church.

Many Christians (between 75 and 90 percent of them) credit a friend or a family member with leading them to Christ. Less than 1 percent credit crusades, and 6 to 8 percent credit a church ministry; 4 to 5 percent credit a pastor.[1]

But even as most Christians are won to Christ by individuals they know, many people are turned off to Christ by people they know. People can also be turned off by groups of people (like small groups and churches).

Imagine that you are absorbed in examining four-door sedans in a used-car lot. A salesperson approaches. Absorbed in your quest, you don't pay too much attention to his arrival. But when he gets close to you, your senses command your attention. That smell! An unpleasant body odor emanates from him. As he smiles, you try to pretend that nothing is wrong. Then your senses are assaulted afresh: bad breath and the worst set of teeth you have ever seen. As you focus your attention on him, you see that his tie does not match his clothes. His pants are "high waters." His shirt is rumpled. His hair is uncombed.

Would you purchase a car from this individual? Or would you seek out a different salesperson or even a different lot?

So it is with our faith. Colossians 3 instructs us to deposit our sinful tendencies in the garbage while clothing ourselves with God's "lifestyle threads" (a paraphrase, of course!). Bad attitudes, gossip, cynicism and crude jokes are about as appropriate to a Christian as long underwear is to a swimmer or as shorts are to a cross-country skier.

Group Witness

Just as individual lifestyle is important to our witness, so is our group lifestyle. In fact, group witness can be either more persuasive or more alienating than an individual's witness. Consider the following list of reasons individuals give for not attending church and/or not following Jesus:

☐ Christians are snobbish.

☐ I went to that church and they were cold.

☐ All churches do is gossip and fight.

☐ I went to a group and all they did was complain about the pastor.

☐ I was emotionally abused by that pastor and some of the board members and leaders.

☐ I tried to ask them to help me with a particular sin, and they judged me instead.

Not all criticism directed at the church is reasonable. And on judgment day God will certainly not accept such criticism as a reason for rejecting God. Nevertheless, we need to listen to the criticism. Jesus' saying that "where two or three are gathered together in my name, there am I in the midst of them" speaks to the dynamic presence of God. Then may not the opposite also be true: where two or three are gathered in his name there is tremendous power for harm and abuse.

It is essential that seekers and believers enter the church through a safe location that will nurture them and equip them to grow. A SAFE group is one that *shares* personal stories, *articulates* its faith, *fosters* dynamic lifestyle ministry and *encourages* intergroup caring.

Shares Personal Stories

Almost every Bible study resource on the market includes sections meant to acquaint group members with one another and to encourage community building. Most accomplish this by asking "past, present and future" questions. There are many good reasons to start a group meeting with community building: (1) it gets people talking about their favorite topic (themselves); (2) it can help to set up the session's lesson by focusing the questions in a particular direction (for example, a session on time management might begin with several community-building questions about different aspects of participants' time) and (3) it opens people up to the idea that they may need change in their lives.

Unfortunately, many groups unknowingly miss the real reason for such questions. The purpose of community building is to lead a group into a deeper level of caring. Such caring is not created through gathering information or telling humorous stories. There is a revelatory act, present in deeper levels of sharing, that is missing from many groups.

To illustrate, consider the various levels on which we interact with one another. There is the "Hi, how are you?" level in which we merely greet each other. The next level, "What's happening?" involves conversing about the weather or a busy schedule. A deeper level, "What's going on with your life?" involves perhaps complaining about taxes or griping about a demanding spouse.

The next level—the "What is concerning you about your life?" level—is one attained by many groups: we learn to share real situations in our lives. We are struggling with foot problems, high bills or job concerns. This level of sharing informs our prayers for and about one another.

As we grow spiritually in our group life, we should begin to go beyond the comfortable questions about our hobbies, stresses and gripes and begin to address fears, personality characteristics, feelings and troublesome sin areas. A group that is not sharing at those levels is merely scratching at the surface of real human interaction.

This level of sharing is significant in witness. If we don't allow God to work in our lives now, we can only testify to what God has done in our lives in the past. Our words about God's grace and power become, perhaps unknown to us, empty and devoid of meaning. We miss the dynamic involved in deep, rich conversation that says, "I was blind but now I see."

The SAFE group understands that it invites people in Christ to a relationship involving both God and the community of faith. Real things happen here: sin is exposed and destroyed, pain is identified and healed, oppression is broken and fear is faced and removed.

How does a group go about sharing *personal* stories that reveal God's work in people's lives? First, we can interject "real" questions into group life. An opener question might be, What is happening in your life right now? An application question might be, How can we pray for you in light of our time together?

Second, we can foster a listening approach (instead of a judging approach) to group life. This means that group members who like to solve every problem need to lighten up. We can encourage people to use the *I* word instead of the *you* word. Using the *I* word ("this is what I hear" or "this is how I feel based on what you are saying") keeps us from trying to fix each other's problems. We learn to listen and pray, trusting the Spirit of God to lead each of us to deeper levels. Jettisoning the judging approach encourages people to grow in trust and to open more of their lives to God's work. The Spirit is then able to do a significant work, and God receives the glory for positive changes.

Imagine a newcomer entering a group that couples a deep level of interaction with a healthy way of conversing. He will be given opportunity to listen to individual and group stories about God's grace. He can then make his own choices about opening up and growing. As he moves through the levels of communication, the group can listen patiently and wait while God does a good work in his life.

Articulates Its Faith

Many groups prefer superficial conversation because it feels safe. But in such a climate the flame of God's love begins to grow dim. God's Spirit does not operate in small, safe, close confines. Rather, the Spirit prefers the wide-open spaces of humility and shared learning.

Faith and a sense of God's presence grow in the atmosphere of a caring community. Groups that are stagnant or apathetic, for whom the Bible has ceased to be alive, need to begin sharing personal stories in an authentic manner. Then as a hunger for God grows, they must begin feeding their souls with real spiritual food—Scripture.

Unfortunately, human beings have an amazing ability to remove themselves in a subtle way from the learning process, for example, by praying for God to change a difficult group member; by knowing so much that everyone looks to you for answers; by answering questions related to the study but never asking what God needs to do in our lives and by unconsciously assuming that our faith is mature because we follow many of the basic behavioral norms of Christianity (I don't smoke or chew, I don't go to movies, drink or cheat on my spouse and so on).

Small groups can be shallow. They may produce an atmosphere of support and caring, but they often do not grapple with deeper questions about themselves, God or the world. They unknowingly inoculate themselves against the very thing they want more than anything.

What does it mean for a small group to articulate its faith? What can a SAFE group do to help its members stay on the cutting edge of growth?

The attitude that creates articulated faith is humility. Humility creates a restless desire to know God and to put oneself in the way of spiritual growth. Humility is not content with simple answers or perfect statements of faith. It wants to know, to learn, to interact and, above all, to change.

One survey of Christian leaders discovered that leaders who remain sharp and focused in ministry think theologically, meaning that they focus on knowing God better as they age. This trait puts them in contrast with people who have everything figured out at an early age and feel no need for any more discussion (or interaction, learning or problem solving).

Articulating faith is important for a group wanting to involve itself in mission because seekers learn best in an atmosphere of seeking. If the group organizes its study to accommodate a newcomer but some group members consider themselves beyond a study of Jesus (just think about that for a minute!), then the seeker will shut down. Those who continuously search for new insight and blessing will have a much more positive witness.

How can a group keep itself on the cutting edge of faith? Here are a few ideas. First, it can choose materials less on the basis of familiarity ("we've used these resources before and we really enjoy them") and more on the basis of the challenges they present. Second, it can inventory its growth needs, focusing its learning time on issues that members need to be challenged by. Third, it can ask questions such as, What does God want to do in your life right now? and then have each person answer them.

Fosters Dynamic Lifestyle Ministry

We Americans have learned to compartmentalize our lives into private life (family, leisure), public life (work, volunteer activities) and worship life (church and service). We do this for several reasons. First, modern culture encourages this kind of segmenting. Instead of perceiving life as an integrated whole, we may, for example, read books about various aspects of our lives, which we then work on. Second, many of us lead uprooted lives. In the days of the Waltons, the private, the public and the church aspects of life ran together seamlessly, if for no other reason than people lived together in the same community for generations. Third, compartmentalizing allows us to gain control of at least one area of life and thus feel better about ourselves.

But this approach to life is not biblical, since we are (always) the temple of God's Spirit, we are (always) part of God's family and we are (always) to do everything to the glory of God. It is dangerous to speak of outreach as a separate activity, as if it were something that could be separated from the rest of God's activity. It cannot be. An outreaching group is motivated by God's love and care. People who are motivated by God's love care at all times.

Caring groups know how to give. And they care regardless of circumstances. When members learn about a family that has lost its home to a fire, they quietly collect blankets and clothes. When they hear that a woman is traveling every day to care for her dying mother and needs help with her children, they volunteer to babysit. A group member reads about a situation of need in Rwanda and begins praying about it daily (while considering her own response). These are people through whom God can work: groups that are community (share their personal stories), groups that search the depths of God's wisdom and grace (articulate their faith) and groups that give without being told that it is something they must do (foster dynamic lifestyle ministry). Such a group is a SAFE place for seekers.

To begin fostering a ministry mindset, your group can begin to treat life callings and jobs as ministries instead of impositions. Instead of complaining about work associates, pray for them. Instead of commiserating together on the difficulties of the modern work world, pray about making a greater difference.

There are, of course, many other ways to encourage ministry in and through the group: listening for needs that arise in the church or the community, volunteering at a soup kitchen or performing a service project (some ideas are presented in later chapters).

Groups that do not share miss out on the experience of receiving God's blessing and passing it on. But when you invite a newcomer into a group whose members know how to give and receive love, you will observe the great things that can happen.

Encourages Intragroup Caring

The listening, seeking, ministry-oriented group needs to care for itself. This point may seem obvious to some, but not all groups are oriented toward caring.

First, a caring group learns to forgive, openly if possible. Shared life proceeds either toward confession of sin (for my negative impact on the world) or toward forgiveness of sin (for the world's negative impact on me). A caring group does not negate pain or sweep differences under the rug. Instead, "speaking the truth in love," it encourages honest interaction and deep levels of forgiveness.

Second, a caring group is attuned to what is happening in the lives of its members. The group's greatest witness to the world lies in caring for its members. When one member's car breaks down, another member goes out of his way to help. When a member is sick in the hospital, the group visits the hospitalized one and takes meals to her family. When a member is experiencing depression, the group sits with him through many hours of prayer and listening.

Third, a caring group welcomes God's power as its members forgive, listen and respond. They feel that they can make a difference. They know that they can make choices. They are in control. Caring groups empower members to be servants, and servanthood is the highest expression of citizenship in God's kingdom.

Such groups are a SAFE place to be.

The Conclusion of the Matter

I have known congregations and groups that played games. Manipulation was a part of every relationship. People's time and energy went into protecting their turf and their image. When churches and groups like this attempt to do ministry, things do not work well. Their witness appears stiff and unreal.

I have also known congregations and groups that invested heavily in building community and a sense of ministry. These congregations love from the inside out. Their environment is genuine and their work is powerful.

Christians and groups will never capture the power of witness until they accept the love of the body and allow God's grace to permeate and sweep through the deepest recesses of their souls. Groups that comport themselves in a SAFE manner will find that they are ministering to seekers and each member is growing as the body builds itself up in love.

2

Developing an Out-Reaching Vision

The Wednesday-evening Bible study group had been together for six years. During that time members had studied various books of the Bible as well as some popular Christian authors. But then group members began to feel a need for change. For some time the group had been growing lethargic. Members were coming late and were not doing their homework. Meetings meandered along without focus. After discussing a broad range of possibilities, members decided to develop an outward focus. They identified changes that needed to be made in the group's communication and life pattern in order to welcome newcomers. And then members began to invite their friends.

The College Ministry Fellowship at First Church ministered to college students from the nearby university. Although the core of the group had remained strong, the group had not grown. Finally members met to brainstorm ways of reaching out to spiritually hungry college students on their campus. In the course of the discussion, group leaders realized that most of the fellowship members had little or no contact with nonbelievers. The group began to pray for an evangelistic heart, and then it held a second brainstorming session. Group members decided to hold dorm pizza gatherings, evangelistic Bible studies, service projects and evangelism training events. Then the group began to grow.

The problems highlighted by these scenarios are not uncommon in the small group setting. Spiritual hunger is at an all-time high, yet the church of Jesus Christ has not effectively mobilized its small groups to reach out beyond themselves and grow. While groups bond well and care deeply, they seem to encounter difficulty in growing and in caring for people beyond their group.

Small groups are spread throughout the cultural landscape, touching all ages, generations, cultures and economic groups. According to a Gallup study of American small groups conducted by Robert Wuthnow of Princeton University, about 40 percent of adult Americans currently belong to groups, many of them church-related. These groups meet a variety of needs in a phenomenal grassroots movement that has received very little attention from either secular or Christian media.[1]

Yet the cultural impact of small groups has been relatively weak. The small group movement "is succeeding less because it is bucking the system than because it is going with the flow. It does not offer a form of community that can be gained only at great social or personal cost. Instead, it provides a kind of social interaction that busy, rootless people can grasp without making significant adjustments in their lifestyles."[2]

On the one hand, the small group movement has unbelievable potential; on the other hand, its impact is less than impressive. How can we encourage groups to become more ministry oriented? How can we reverse our natural preoccupation with ourselves and our needs? How can we touch the hearts of groups and their members to consider the plight of the unsaved? How can we motivate our people for service, outreach and justice?

The Vision

There are many ways to address the problems of ingrown small groups. We can educate groups and leaders about the need that exists. We can create training videos and other resources to stimulate service and outreach. We can encourage churches and campus ministries to set goals for growth. We can even use guilt as a motivational technique. Each of these techniques may have its place as we attempt to reconfigure the small group movement into a tool for outreach.

A better approach, however, is to start offering a vision. Great movements in history always start with a vision. Vision provides a snapshot of our final destination. Vision provides the motives (such as faith, hope and love) necessary to take risks and accomplish great things. Vision flows from the mind of God into our hearts, spurring us to action. And vision draws God's people to invest significant time in prayer, allowing us to tap into God's power for effective ministry.

I recall my early involvement with small groups. I was influenced by church leaders such as LeRoy Eims, Robert Coleman and Paul Yonggi

---

Vision: What Benefits Can Small Groups Bring to a Church?

1. Energized disciples
2. Growing Christians
3. Praying individuals and groups
4. Assimilated newcomers
5. Individualized ministry
6. Deep level of member care
7. Flexibility to change and adapt with the times
8. Individuals encouraged to learn and use their gifts
9. Effective, nonthreatening outreach
10. Deep relationships

Cho about the potential impact of small groups on the church and the world. Early disciplemakers offered the vision of one person leading to Christ and nurturing two persons each year, those two persons then leading to Christ and nurturing two persons per year and so on. In such a scenario the world would be won to Christ in about thirty years, without large crusades or mass evangelism. That vision struck a chord with me that has fueled my continued interest in small groups.

As an example of what small groups can do, Paul Yonggi Cho's church in Seoul, South Korea, has grown to over five hundred thousand people and is larger than many denominations. This church grows because the small groups in it do outreach.

Big-Picture Vision and Little-Picture Vision

If we are to successfully engage small groups in Western culture, we must cultivate a vision. Vision for small group outreach needs to take both the big picture and the small picture into account.

In the big picture, try to imagine what would happen if one-third (one million of the three million existing groups estimated by Wuthnow in the Gallup study) of the small groups in America prayed for and led at least one person to Christ each year. In the first year, the results would be one million new lives touched for Christ. But the impact does not end there. Since the new believers would be saved in the context of a faith community, discipleship would already be built into the process (saving local churches time, staffing and money).

Consider the impact that the new believers could make. Each new believer has relational contacts that include nonbelievers. The (nurtured) new believer becomes salt and light to a segment of the world that the church may not be touching. Further, the new believer tends to bring hunger and excitement to groups (which may include older believers), stimulating growth and encouraging deeper risk.

To these changes add the *cultural* impact of at least one million new believers being led to Christ and nurtured each year. Within ten years the social, cultural, relational and spiritual landscape of America would be touched profoundly (perhaps a grassroots revival).

Vision for small groups in the small picture involves their impact on the local community of faith. For example, imagine a church with a regular attendance of two hundred. The church (including adult Sunday school and choir) has ten adult groups. If half of those groups led five people to faith in Christ and if *all* of the groups participated regularly in service evangelism activities (see chapter nine), the church would experience dynamic growth. Consider how five baby Christians could enliven an established church.

But a vision for outreach does not take shape easily, and changes in group life that it requires do not occur spontaneously. Vision arises within the context of our expectations, unconscious actions, dreams and presuppositions. Visionary eyes, which enable you to see into the future, need to look to the present and address your personal and small group strengths and weaknesses. Implementing a group's dream requires a patient, transitional approach, which is highlighted in the rest of this chapter.

The Problem

Have you ever visited the home of a someone who prevailed on you to do (or eat) something against your will? For example, "Of course you will want another serving of my raspberry spinach soufflé; everybody loves it!" Or "I know you'll enjoy looking through our children's picture albums." Or "You can't leave yet; we haven't even begun to scratch the surface of my childhood."

A gift offered in an inappropriate manner or with self-centered carelessness is usually not appreciated. Effective gift givers are thoughtful, caring and sensitive. They know how to perceive the right time and place, and they make giving and receiving a positive experience.

Christians have a gift to give. Scripture calls it the "good news": human beings can be reconciled to God and to one another through Jesus. We live in a world filled with hostility and broken relationships. Through God those relationships are reoriented and are made whole.

We must think carefully about how to give away the good news, bearing in mind that there are many ways for a group to fumble outreach. Your demeanor can be harsh. Your message can be garbled. You can, unknowingly, shut out the very people you think you are inviting in. Inviting people to join the group may cause resentment among some group members, who may try to sabotage new relationships before they have a chance to develop.

So groups need to learn how to turn bad habits into positive, vision-nurturing activities. In the rest of this chapter we will look at six outreach-inhibiting habits and will discuss ways to make the group more outreach friendly.

Moving from Cozy to Welcoming

Imagine walking with a friend into a room filled with people you have never met. As soon as you enter the room, your one friend is deluged with hugs, animated conversation and a host of inside jokes. Every now and then a person moves your way, seemingly out of obligation. After a short, stilted conversation you are again on your own.

This is a scenario that many find unappealing. We dislike feeling ignored. We need to feel a sense of belonging. Created in the image of God, we have a deep longing for attachment to an eternal community. We are injured when our human community ignores us or does not consider our needs.

Herein lies a significant pitfall for many groups. Over time groups become close, familiar and cozy. They share experiences that induce laughter, especially when certain familiar phrases and experiences are called to mind. A close group develops its own language, thought patterns and habits. A newcomer to such an environment can feel frozen out. Perhaps she utters a phrase and everyone laughs. A member leans over and explains, "Inside joke." She may wonder at whose expense the joke was made.

A group that wants to do outreach needs to take serious inventory of its welcoming character. It needs to consider (in advance) how to handle such issues as inside jokes (can we include the newcomer in our laughter?), group language (will we explain what we are doing next, and why?), group stories and shared experiences (can we stop trying to prove how close we are and concentrate on welcoming the newcomer?) and group posture (how can we communicate, by our attention, body language and seating arrangement, that we value people attempting to enter our group?). By considering such issues in advance of newcomers, you can raise group awareness, become more sensitive and intentionally plan to be a welcoming group.

Moving from Head to Heart
As groups build community and study together, many want to move beyond simple teaching and study complex issues. When the group was getting started, it may have used a small group starter resource (like *Small Group Starter Kit,* published by InterVarsity Press). The group may have gone on to use a basics of the faith resource and from

there to a few Bible studies and a relational study. Hunger for learning may then direct members to a more intensive Bible study resource and perhaps a book on the attributes of God.

These studies are of great benefit to Christian growth and worship. However, the group that does outreach and invites people to join needs to realize that people being touched by the gospel may need a simpler learning environment.

For example, a group that invites a newcomer in the middle of a Revelation study may promptly lose the member. A group that invites a newcomer to a study of Christ based on the Gospel of Mark has a greater chance of succeeding. And the group that not only invites a newcomer but includes the newcomer in the learning process, *while* exhibiting great curiosity and spiritual hunger, has the greatest chance for assimilating a new member.

If the group includes a philosopher or a theologian who likes to hear himself discourse on various topics, it needs to rein in that person before he can do some real harm. People opening their hearts to the Spirit do not need to be discouraged by a headstrong person or a group that is subconsciously bent on showing off its knowledge.

How can you move from head to heart as a group? First, if you are not taking time in each group meeting to listen to each other and to express genuine love, then you need to focus more time on building group relationships. Second, as you prepare to invite people, it will be helpful to ask the question, Does our group environment encourage people to "sermonize" and present themselves as having all the right answers? And third, you might want to look through youth ministry or small group resources for a listening role-play or game that encourages active listening instead of active talking. Finally, you may choose a simple study when inviting newcomers so that genuine seeking can occur in a safe environment.

Moving from Haphazard to Intentional

I once participated in a group that included one "missionary." Several other members of that group were reluctant to allow new people to attend. But not the missionary. He would frequently bring a new person to our meetings, creating discomfort for members who had not given him permission to do that. The resentment in the group atmosphere finally discouraged newcomers from attending at all.

Such an approach to outreach is counterproductive—ineffective and even harmful. Every outreach event or group newcomer in some sense creates a crisis. Dynamics and feelings must be considered. Plans must be made. Group members must be consulted.

Group consensus is the best way to avoid haphazard planning. Groups that operate according to consensus do only what every member wants to do. One dissenting vote can trigger a compromise or a rejection of new ideas. Group consensus is healthy in that every member is valued as part of the planning process and each member owns the outcome. Those who express a willingness to try something are expected to follow through.

Some of the planning issues related to outreach include (1) whether we want to do outreach, (2) what kind of outreach is best for our group, (3) what each member's participation will be and (4) how we can minimize potential drawbacks and pitfalls. If your group is not yet sold on the idea of outreach, it is a good idea to discuss the four points just listed.

Moving from Static to Dynamic

Well-established groups have their own rhythm and life. Their group life is, to them, quite normal and comfortable. Why should they bother to explain their actions to a newcomer? After all, anybody can see that this group is functioning quite well!

But even well-functioning groups need to consider outreach dynamics. Otherwise, a newcomer may well think, *They are doing well without me. Why should I stay?*

The best way for a happy, healthy group to welcome a newcomer is to show that it values her. You may consider pairing her with a secure group member who can communicate well and can give her the knowledge and security she needs to thrive in the group. The partner (or group) can then explain the purpose of the group and how it goes about its business (best communicated through a group covenant). By going over the group covenant and making sure that she has a group study guide (if necessary), you can communicate important information about the group in an efficient manner. The person will feel valued and the group will assimilate newcomers well.

Moving from Dysfunction to Wholeness

Some groups should not participate in outreach—for example, a group that is racked by dissension, a group that includes an unhealthy member who drains the group's emotional life, a gossip who betrays confidences or a couple that fights openly. In these cases the best outreach plan is an "inreach" plan.

Dysfunctional groups need to learn how to function well in community before they attempt to share what they have with others. Some groups feel that defining a mission will make these kinds of problems go away. Not quite. The best that such a group can hope to do is lead a licensed, trained therapist to Christ, who can then help the group get healthy! Short of that scenario (which is presented tongue in cheek), another person added to the dysfunctional group will only become involved in its destructive group system.

The dysfunctional group needs to build community. Perhaps it should plan fun events to get its members laughing and enjoying one another's company. Or it may benefit from consulting a resource on conflict resolution so that it can lay its tensions to rest. If it has valued task (such as Bible study) over maintenance (such as community building), it should allocate time for people to share what is going on with them. Once the group has identified and addressed its problems, it can minister to others.

Moving from Self-Centeredness to Other-Centeredness

Some small groups have built deep community over the years, praying their members through significant trials and learning much about the Bible through study.

Unfortunately, the longer a group is together without any sense of call to a larger body—whether to church or society—the more removed the group becomes from those who need what it has to offer. Perhaps out of fear or just plain frustration, many Christians and groups have engaged in cocooning, removing themselves from the world and its problems. In the long run, however, a person's or a group's growth is stunted by a lack of practical ministry.

The self-centered group should cultivate, through prayer and study, hunger for outreach. There are many books and videos (for example, *Becoming a Contagious Christian* by Bill Hybels, Zondervan) that direct a group to issues related to sharing its faith. As it studies, the group should ask God to give its members a heart for others.

Study and prayer are not the end but the beginning. These groups should then plan and implement an outreach ministry that includes others in the group's blessing.

Where to Start

Many groups are seeking to do outreach. If your group is one of them, you might be wondering why this chapter on vision takes a look at bad habits that your group may have. What does this have to do with vision?

The Gospel of Mark begins with the words "the *beginning* of the gospel ['good news'] of Jesus Christ." Then it tells the story of John the baptizer, who was used by God to prepare the way for Christ. Ironically, John told people to repent. As people came to the desert and confessed their sin, they were prepared to receive Jesus Christ. Thus the "good news" began with the "bad news."

The "bad news-before-good news" principle is where we begin our journey. Self-satisfied dysfunction or blind ignorance can block our path to ministry. We must confess the sins of self-centeredness and isolation that have hampered our witness to the world. Only by naming individual sins as well as group sins will we begin addressing our problems, with the help of God.

As you prayerfully embrace a vision and as you consider the group weaknesses listed in this chapter, you begin traveling the road of outreach.

3

Groups
That Invite

In 1979 I traveled with a Christian singing group, the Continental Singers. Beginning our trip in California, we traveled across the United States and ultimately spent a few weeks in Eastern Europe (including East Germany and Poland). Finally we made our way back across the United States, ending in California. It was an exciting experience for me, since my international travel had previously been limited to Canada.

I was not attracted to the tour because I had a burning desire to participate in evangelistic ministry for Jesus. In fact, ministry was the farthest thing from my mind. What I wanted was adventure, and Eastern Europe promised unpredictability. In high school I had read books about daring Brother Andrew smuggling Bibles into Communist countries, and I thought it would be fun to attempt something similar.

As part of our tour group training in California, we received instruction on how to guide others to Jesus. But I had no interest in evangelistic training. It was not part of my past church experience, so it held little value for me. Why spend time preparing to sit down with a needy person and go through a little booklet together?

I regretted not paying more attention once the tour was under way. After each concert we tore down the concert equipment and loaded up our bus. I especially enjoyed that part of the tour, sharing the role with my friends Paul and Matt. But one aspect of the postconcert ritual made me nervous. Each evening the tour director chose several individuals to watch for people who raised their hands during the commitment time. These "chosen few" were to strike up conversations with those who raised their hands and look for an opportunity to lead them to Christ.

When I was posted as one of the "chosen few," I would stand as unobtrusively as possible in a corner of the sanctuary. Filled with fear, I prayed—that nobody would have the audacity to come near me. When a person seemed to be approaching me, I would pick up a leftover brochure and begin reading.

My strategy worked for much of the summer. But one hundred days is a long time to hide, and finally someone actually cornered me. As I recall, my tour director, with a teenager in tow, grabbed me by the arm and sat us down together. I looked at the person with terror in my eyes.

In that moment I confronted the source of my fear: insecurity. I realized that I was unwilling to talk to people because I did not know how to care. Slowly, we began to talk. He haltingly answered my questions about his family and past. Eventually we got around to Jesus, and I told him what little I could. I still remember how painfully the word *Jesus* rolled off my tongue. It was an entirely unfamiliar part of my vocabulary. I felt awkward talking about someone I was supposed to know deeply but appeared to know only in passing.

In spite of my self-perceived mumbling and stumbling, the young person invited Jesus into his heart and, I presume, began a new life. But he was not the only person who changed on that evening. I changed. I became an evangelist. God's desire began to take root in my life. I began to tell others about Jesus because I had tasted the sweet honey of salvation. It was a defining moment that I almost missed because of fear.

Send Reinforcements!

The vast majority Christians have never had an opportunity to lead someone to Christ. Although some church leaders may blame them for being apathetic, I believe that insecurity is the root cause.

Pastor Steve Sjogren labels one-on-one evangelism "high risk/high grace" (see chapter nine of this book for a full explanation of Sjogren's ideas about service evangelism).[1] The risk in sharing one's beliefs with another person is that it requires a level of faith that many have not attained.

There are several ways to respond to the risks. The first is to make witnesses in training "bite the bullet" as I did in my first encounters.

Reasons People Fear Evangelism—and How Groups Can Help

Fear	Small Group Benefit
1. How will I get the courage to speak?	Teamwork
2. What will I say?	Group support
3. At what point do I share?	Invitation to a group event
4. How will I get this person to church?	Comfort/security of a home
5. What if I'm not a great Christian?	Power of group prayer
6. What if the person becomes a Christian?	Group nurture and encouragement

---

This approach has some merit, although many will not allow themselves to be put in such a position. Sending people out on the streets to engage in one-on-one evangelistic interaction can seem forced and artificial.

The second way to respond to evangelism's risk is to call in reinforcements. Reversing the "go it alone" mentality of many Western cultures, Christians are discovering strength in numbers.

According to this method of addressing (not negating) evangelism's risks, a team of people (let's call them a small group) decides to evangelize their friends. Perhaps they begin by praying for several individuals they hope to bring into their group. They may study a resource that empowers them to discuss their faith openly. Then they invite one non-Christian friend (or possibly more) to join them. They create an opportunity, in partnership with the Spirit of God, to share Jesus with their friends.

Serendipity founder Lyman Coleman calls this "side door evangelism." It allows seekers to avoid the front door of a church (figuratively speaking), where visitors often enter in full view of all of the established members. Instead, people are allowed to question, probe, learn and open their hearts in a caring small group environment. It is the most effective means of direct evangelism that exists.

The Importance of Group Evangelism

Churches that plan to grow as the second millennium closes will either adopt the side-door technique of group evangelism or prepare to die. There are two simple reasons for this: (1) baby boomers and (2) Generation Xers (of course, other generations can also benefit from small group evangelism).

Baby boomers have been returning to church, although not in the record numbers some had anticipated. As they return, they bring a number of cultural distinctives. They tend to distrust organizations (including the established church and church denominations). Their mobility makes them feel disconnected. They crave authentic relationships.

Generation Xers may distrust organizations more than baby boomers do. Growing up in a time of high change, high mobility, high technology and a high rate of societal failure (evidenced in a downsized government, rewritten welfare mandates and moral failures of high-profile religious and political leaders, among others), they need an authentic "someone" to embrace. They are not often attracted to glitzy, impressive programs. They are put off by backslapping and alligator smiles.

These demographic groups will not be transformed through radio or television programming (although they can help) and will not be reached effectively through mass tract efforts. In what might be a return to New Testament evangelistic techniques, they need a human touch, a caring community and the opportunity to ask questions without being given glib answers.

To these two generations especially, small group evangelism offers a healing salve. Created to connect intimately with God and one another, individuals can reconnect with their God-given call (to "come home") in small groups.

Small group evangelism offers another alternative to front-door, build-it-and-they-will-come efforts that have occupied the church's evangelistic attention for generations.

Evangelism Options for Small Groups

Jim worked in a large office building and for several years had been meeting with a small group of men weekly over lunch. The group had become strong, and a number of men's lives had been enhanced through the regular spiritual interaction.

Over time, the individual prayer requests had begun centering around work situations involving group members' associates. So Jim, in a sudden burst of inspiration, included requests for the salvation of work associates during the prayer time.

The prayers revolutionized the way that the men approached their work. Group members began to find tangible ways to share God's grace with others. Those who were bosses became more understanding; those who experienced tension in relationships began to soften. Eventually, several of those they were praying for began attending the group, and they came to faith.

Groups that adopt the "strength in numbers" approach to evangelism have a number of options available to them. They can set aside several weeks or months of group time each year to invite non-Christian friends. Or they can invite non-Christian friends to join them at any time during the year. Or they can become a support group studying issues relevant to people in their demographic group. Or they can become a recovery group offering healing from one or more dysfunctions common in society (more on each of these issues later in this chapter). They may even want to take more dramatic approaches like becoming an evangelistic group, penetrating a different local culture (crosscultural) or offering seminars that become evangelistic groups. (This subject is discussed in chapter eight.)

Praying

Preparing your group for evangelism requires addressing several issues.

The first issue to be addressed is prayer. In the past decade or so I have led many small groups. While the emphasis varied from group to group, they all had one thing in common. After the group had been meeting for at least four months, members brainstormed a list of several friends who needed to know Jesus Christ. We committed to praying for those individuals in the months to come (typically late winter to early summer).

I have noticed that the individuals and the groups who diligently pray in this manner experience subtle but dramatic changes. Their public presence softens and they become more willing to listen. Their witness becomes more vibrant. Although we encourage individuals not to discuss their faith openly during our months of prayer, they become better witnesses.

We pray partly to encourage the Spirit of God to soften our friends' hearts. We pray mostly because the Spirit of God will soften our hearts.

So prayer as a strategy is not to be taken lightly. We do not know when or how God will answer our prayers for the salvation of family and friends. Decades may elapse before the prayers take root and grow.

But *we* experience change as we invest our prayers and lives in seeking the salvation of others. Any group that anticipates evangelism in the next year will benefit by setting aside time each week (and encouraging individuals in the group to set aside time each day) for intercession.

Gathering Information and Sharing Fears

Groups preparing to share Jesus need to become acquainted with the idea of sharing Jesus. The word *Jesus* rolled uncomfortably off my tongue the first time I shared my faith. Others may experience similar problems. To allay members' concerns, it may be helpful for a group to set aside a number of weeks to study issues related to witnessing.

Many book and video resources exist to help groups examine witnessing issues. But studying a resource is just part of the equation. Sharing openly our fears, desires, dreams and concerns, and addressing them in prayer, is part of this step as well. Few Christians need to be convinced to witness. What we need is encouragement and an environment that challenges us to face our fears and overcome our insecurities.

Some groups may even decide to have a practice session, where "Christians" attempt to articulate their faith to "non-Christians" in the group. Most people learn best through hands-on training and problem solving.

Talking to Your Relational Network

The greatest selling point in small group ministry is the "salted" curiosity of people who see us growing and wonder why, including friends, family members and coworkers. It is also true of your congregation. People tend to flock to something that works well.

Your Relational Network—Who Might Benefit from Small Groups?

When you think about people you might invite to a small group, have you considered the following?
1. Your immediate family
2. Your extended family
3. Your neighbors
4. Your closest friends
5. Your acquaintances
6. Your work associates
7. Your church family

In chapter two we discussed the importance of your small group's being a healthy community. Many people crave the authenticity of agape love. One aspect of evangelism preparation is making use of opportunities to speak about the benefits you receive from being in a group, possibly including what Jesus means to you.

As you and your group prepare for evangelism, each individual should sit down with a pen and paper. List family, friends, neighbors and work associates. To identify the people your group should pray for and talk to, look for the ones who (1) live close enough to attend the group, (2) need the life-giving offer of salvation through Jesus and (3) would be comfortable in your group.

Choosing an Option

Next you need to decide how to structure your group for outreach (see additional discussion in chapter four). Taking into account your group's strengths and weaknesses, you must choose the option that best suits you. There are several choices. First, you can pray for and invite non-Christian friends at any time during the year. Some very special groups have a gift for evangelism. No matter what they study, people can enter and feel comfortable. They care, they communicate, they love and they listen, all within the context of group life. This first option is a choice for groups with mature (not merely knowledgeable) Christians who know how to show love in action.

Second, you can pray for and invite non-Christian friends at special times during the year. A life cycle approach to small group ministry suggests that groups (1) build community in the fall, (2) learn, study and worship in the winter, (3) empower and train members in the spring and (4) do outreach in the late spring or early summer. According to this option the group essentially reconstitutes itself for outreach and evangelism sometime late in the school calendar year.

One way to approach this option is to study Jesus during this time. The Gospel of Mark gives a clear, fast-paced introduction to Jesus. The Gospel of John presents a clear apologetic for Christ's divinity and ability to save. There are study materials that specifically focus on the person of Jesus.

Another way to approach this option is to become a support group. Support group materials (for example, a resource dealing with stress) make a wonderful evangelistic tool because (1) they get people talking about themselves, (2) they help people identify a source of pain in their lives and (3) and they draw people—in a nonthreatening manner—to address what Scripture has to say about their problems.

Yet another way to approach this option is to become a recovery group. Recovery groups are much more intense than support groups and much more focused on self-destructive behavior (for example, alcoholism) or life-altering situations (for example, the death of a child or a terminal illness). Recovery groups should be offered under the supervision of an informed, professional ministry.

Handling Logistics

The next step is careful reflection on your group logistics. Specifically, you will want to consider meeting location(s), room layout, meeting schedules and covenant demands.

Many small groups rotate their meeting location among members' homes. This poses a difficulty to newcomers. Practice suggests that newcomers will not attend something new that is difficult to locate (parking included). If you normally rotate meetings, it may be important to meet at one member's home for the first four meetings. Also, arrange to meet newcomers at a "friendly" location (such as a fast-food restaurant) and let them follow you to the meeting. Knowing that someone may be waiting for them, they will be less prone to "chicken out."

Room layout poses similar problems. If you have become accustomed to a barking dog, noisy children and a ringing telephone, then you may not realize how difficult these distractions may be for a newcomer. He or she is already insecure and does not need unwelcome interruptions. You may choose to relocate to a quieter location until the newcomer is more relaxed.

The meeting schedule may need consideration. For example, your meetings may end with an hour of sharing and praying. While you may want to retain these elements, the time can be shortened. If you don't include refreshments or time for community building, you may want to add them. And if your group requires significant home study to prepare for meetings, perhaps you may want to soften the homework by discontinuing it or reducing the amount of it.

Following Through

For the purpose of small group evangelism, salvation may be analyzed as justification (being made right with God), sanctification (growing deeper with God) and glorification (living with God for all eternity). Salvation represents the beginning of an eternal journey as a person grows in the grace and love of God expressed through Jesus Christ.

The small group needs to consider how it will deal with new believers (for example, during a six-week summer layoff). How will it handle problems that a newcomer may bring (for example, a failing marriage or self-destructive behavior)? In many ways, loving a person after salvation is much more challenging than loving a person into salvation.

In preparation for follow-through, you may purchase several basic Christianity resources (either books or studies) so that the person has something to read and study. You may also "assign" one or two group members to call that person regularly, not so much to check up on him as to support him in his new life in Christ.

A Positive First Step

Following chapters include other useful ideas for small group outreach, evangelism and mission. This chapter provides a helpful first step for those groups that want to begin sharing their faith. If your group has never engaged in a form of outreach, you may choose to work the issues presented in this chapter. When you begin to feel comfortable as an inviting group, then it may be time to move on!

4

Groups
That Multiply

Marjorie led a small group composed of women from her congregation. The group experienced a wonderful sense of community, and other women wanted to join. There were a few other small groups in the congregation, but none were as positive as Marjorie's group.

The group wanted to be open and inviting, and so it did not turn away potential newcomers. By the anniversary of its first meeting the group had blossomed from its original five members to fifteen. Several newcomers came from outside the church, and the rest were church members.

Unfortunately, unforeseen difficulties accompanied the growth. Sharing time began to consume most of the meeting, and meetings became quite long. Some women, perhaps thinking they would not be missed in a larger group, began coming late and then began missing meetings entirely. Marjorie did not pick up on the negative results of the group's growth immediately. After all, success can numb the reflective thought processes. After attendance fell to five women for several meetings in a row, Marjorie began to get concerned. Had the growth been illusory? Was she doing something wrong? Was she losing control of the group?

The Problem

From the beginning of the Bible to the end, God's desire is to include more people in his blessing. He told Abraham that all nations on earth would be blessed through his seed (Genesis 12:1-2). Micah 4 contains the powerful image of "many nations" streaming to Zion (Jerusalem, representing God's kingdom and rule). And Jesus told his followers to "make disciples of all peoples" (Matthew 28:18-20).

In the book of Acts, we see God pushing the fledgling church out of Jerusalem, into Judea and Samaria and into the Roman Empire. It was a crisis for the church to move on. They would have preferred the safety of their homes. God had other designs, and so the church was scattered through persecution.

Growth is always a crisis. The history of the church demonstrates that risk and crisis usually accompany growth. Growth breaks into our settled patterns of communication. Growth interrupts the security of deep conversation and stable relationships. Growth requires deep levels of other-centered care.

The alternative to growth, however, is death. A group may exist for five years without experiencing numerical growth. But the group's spiritual growth will begin to stagnate, probably somewhere around year two or three, for the simple reason that knowledge gained becomes stilted in a noninclusive environment. "This is what happens in the process of discipleship. If you are growing in Christ and receiving the benefits of God's blessing, sooner or later God will give you a burden for those who are not saved. . . . And in this we have come full circle. For you see, God's plan is for evangelism and mission to be *the result* of his blessing that comes through study, worship, prayer and community."[1]

Healthy small groups learn to navigate the tension between growth and stagnation. They implement disciplines that prepare them for the stresses of growth. They design systems that provide positive levels of care, allowing people to be heard and valued. And they make the choices that best reflect their call to the church and the community.

Marjorie's group, described at the beginning of the chapter, chose to grow. Unfortunately, it was not successful in addressing the inevitable tensions that accompanied its growth. By changing just a few elements of group life, the group could have grown *and* remained healthy. The rest of the discussion in this chapter reflects on the decisions and choices available to growing groups through revisiting Marjorie's group to understand some of the changes available to it.

The Process of Adding New Members

It may be helpful for you to perceive adding members as a process, not as a one-time step. In church parlance, this process is called assimilation. When you assimilate new members, you talk about why you should invite new members. You decide on a strategy for inviting newcomers, which may include prayer and an open chair. You consider relational networks of friends who might be interested in joining. Before you invite people to join the group, you consider (as a group) what to tell them and how to communicate the group's focus and intent in the invitation. You think through logistics such as how to get them to a meeting (especially if the location is hard to find) and with whom (it is often best for a newcomer to walk into the meeting with a caring friend).

Issues to Address in Member Assimilation (adapted from William Donahue, *The Willow Creek Guide to Leading Life-Changing Small Groups,* **Zondervan)**

Step 1: Before you begin inviting new members, involve everyone in the group in the inviting process. Teach your group about the empty chair, and pray for God to fill the empty chair. Develop a list of potential members.

Step 2: As you start inviting new members, develop relationships prior to the group meeting. Explain the vision of your group to potential members. Ask potential members to pray about joining your group. Allow the person to meet other group members outside of the group. Allow the person to attend a few meetings before making a final commitment.

Step 3: After new members attend the group, affirm the newcomers and those who brought them. Have members briefly retell their own stories. Celebrate what is happening in your group. Be careful not to add people too quickly.

Once a newcomer attends the group, you must continue to communicate your stories (who you are), your covenant and your expectations. Conversations that occur after the meeting may help answer questions, address concerns and minister to any insecurities that the person may be feeling.

If Marjorie's group had employed this process, it could have addressed problems before they arose. They could have spent more time in discussion, considering the persons who were to join, what they were looking for, and how the group might help new members get settled into the disciplines of the group.

Preparing the Group for Multiplication

Growth is not just a choice. It is also an identity. If your group has not consciously chosen to grow, it probably won't grow. So church leaders, most notably those touting "cell" and "meta" small group systems, build growth into the design of small groups. The cell and meta small group systems are strategies that integrate growing small groups into the life of the church.

In the cell system every part of church life happens in a small group. Groups then gather for celebration (worship). Children are nurtured, marriages are strengthened, evangelism and growth are practiced—all in a small group setting.[2]

The meta system is also a small group strategy, but it includes more traditional program elements (for example, a Sunday school). Each structure exists only as it either *acts* in a small group capacity or *feeds* potential members into small groups.[3]

Your group doesn't have to be either type—cell small group or meta small group—in order to grow. But it does need to address the identity and structure issues connected with the nurturing of growth. These issues are most effectively addressed in a positive group covenant (see appendix 2). Here are a few ideas.

First, begin talking about group multiplication from the very beginning of your group life. Several resources that are intended for new groups address issues of multiplication. Among them are *Small Group Starter Kit* by Jeff Arnold (Downers Grove, Ill.: InterVarsity Press, 1994) and *A Pilgrimage Small Group Starter Guide on Community* by Thom Corrigan (Colorado Springs, Colo.: Pilgrimage/NavPress, 1996).

Multiplication needs to be part of your group identity from the time you gather the group. Groups that multiply need to be rewarded. Creativity and initiative need to be encouraged. If Marjorie's group had discussed issues of multiplication early on, it might have been better prepared to cope with the dynamics of growth.

If your group has been meeting for a while but has no growth identity, you may devote a meeting (or a series of meetings) to discuss the importance of being inclusive and inviting. The small group starter resources mentioned above may be adapted to this use.

Second, decide on a structure for growth. There are essentially three structures. Being a closed group means that you never invite newcomers and you never grow. Being an open group means that you always attempt to invite newcomers. Being an open/closed group means combining elements of both. When your group is working through a study or a set of issues, you may remain closed. After you complete the study or work through the issues, you may invite newcomers to join the group.

Marjorie could have benefited from helping her group make this choice. For healthy groups like hers (with potential waiting lists of members), the open/closed group offers the best choice. It allows them to manage the timing of invitations and method of integrating new members.

Third, keep growth issues on the group agenda. Most groups have discovered that the easiest way to encourage growth is to use the "empty chair." This is a chair brought into each meeting and left unoccupied. During prayer time, the group prays for the person who will eventually occupy that chair. This discipline encourages group participants to consider those who can join the group, and it challenges the group to keep growth issues in its thoughts. A good time for the group to pray for the empty chair is at the beginning of the meeting, before relational and personal issues draw attention away from outreach and evangelism.

At first glance, Marjorie's group seemed to employ such disciplines because it grew. But it would have benefited from more prayer and discussion. The members who "voted with their feet" (by not showing up) may have done so because of resentment over growth pressures. If they had concentrated on praying for growth and partnering together in the process, they might have remained strong as new members arrived.

Fourth, think small. Small groups are effective *because* they are small. They focus on the depth of care and conversation necessary to make the church strong, not on activities that are appropriate to large groups. Yet some groups, especially those with ten or more members, grow large without reflecting on what they are losing in the process.

The way around this problem, for growing small groups, is to break into groups of four for part of each meeting. Breaking into smaller groupings, which is helpful when more than seven participants are present, allows the group several luxuries. It prepares you for group multiplication (after all, if you have two "groups" meeting on the same evening, you can meet at separate places or even on separate evenings); it allows you to train an apprentice leader (see below) and it keeps the group small enough to encourage deep sharing and positive care.

Marjorie's group would have benefited from growing by staying small. If Marjorie had apprenticed a leader and had broken the group into several groups for sharing and prayer, the members would probably have felt that their presence was more valued. The level of commitment probably could have been maintained.

Apprenticing Leaders for Multiplication

Leadership "apprenticing" has been discussed by church growth experts for a number of years. Unfortunately, not enough leaders are involved in raising up the next generation of leaders through apprenticing. Perhaps this is because pastors don't often model such mentoring relationships. Or perhaps volunteers are so busy leading a group that they have no time to spend training another leader.

So why should you apprentice leaders? First, because those who apprentice can actually take pressure off themselves. When I apprentice a leader, I do so with the idea of that person's leading the group. The more work I give the apprentice, the easier my job becomes.

Second, because those who apprentice leaders are preparing for growth. The apprentice is put in a position to lead when the group multiplies. You cannot multiply your ministry until you have other leaders who are ready to take on added responsibility.

Third, because those who apprentice leaders have a more dynamic ministry. When leaders interact with others, they place themselves on the cutting edge of personal growth. Mentoring relationships benefit both the leader and the apprentice.

How do you apprentice another leader? First, you pray (you probably guessed that). Second, you choose a leader. If your church has not developed a profile of gifts and personality traits that it desires in small group leaders, you can look for people who are caring, pastoral and respected in the group setting.

Third, you work with the leader. Meet him or her and go over the week's lesson. Demonstrate your method for asking questions and for keeping discussions flowing positively. Take the leader through a leadership training book that can explain leadership issues.

Fourth, you empower. For the good of the group and its apprentice leader, at some point you need to commission him or her for service in the group. Share your willingness to entrust the group to the leader, and begin turning over portions of the meeting to that person. Eventually the new leader can move on to leading whole meetings, as you evaluate his or her preparation and ability to ask positive questions and guide discussion.

Those who empower learn to give responsibility in direct measure to the apprentice's competence and ability to follow through. Apprenticing is not a perfect process. You (and the apprentice) may have overestimated the apprentice's gifts, self-discipline or some other aspect of leadership. The lines of communication (and evaluation) should be open from the very beginning because the process may take longer (in the case of leadership apathy) or terminate altogether (in the case of inability to handle the role).

Fifth, you release. When an apprentice begins to handle responsibility consistently, you may begin praying together about the appropriate method of releasing him or her to a position of leadership. (Several models are discussed later in this chapter.) This moment of release is to be celebrated as a positive step in the life of the person and the group.

Models for Multiplying Groups

When your group has grown by assimilating new members and has prepared for multiplication by apprenticing a leader(s), it may discuss its next steps. Breaking up a group creates a crisis and needs to be done gently. This is not a time for dictatorial commands ("we're going to split our group now!"), but it is not a time for you abdicate your responsibility either ("what do you all think we should do now?"). Instead, you can frame an appropriate statement, possibly, "We have prayed about this moment from the beginning of our group, that we would grow and ultimately find a way to multiply. God has blessed our group, and now we need to discuss some of our options so that we can make an informed, prayerful decision." Such a statement is sensitive yet directive, and it allows you to discuss the options.

There are a several ways to multiply groups. Any one of these models may be employed in any number of situations. There is not necessarily a right way or a wrong way, and one method is not necessarily better than the others.

The first option is the mother-daughter model. The original group remains with the original leader, and the apprentice leaves with the smaller offshoot group. For example, an original group of ten might become two groups, one with six members and the other with four. The strength of this model is that the original group is not overly traumatized. The assumption is that at least some individuals will want to leave with the apprentice.

You may be wondering how a group member chooses which group to join in this scenario. It is possible that everyone will want to remain or that everyone will want to leave. Either possibility creates potential embarrassment.

There are no easy ways around the difficulties. At some point, people need to be given a choice. In many cases persistent patterns in the

---

Models for Group Multiplication

Mother-daughter:	apprentice leaves with members to form new group
Reverse split:	original leader leaves with members to form new group
Apprentice begins new group:	no members leave original group
Leader begins new group:	no members leave original group
Incubation:	leadership training in groups of four
Turbo:	every member of original group leaves to form new group

---

group will determine who remains and who goes. In other cases the original leader may consult with people outside of the group in order to get a handle on the situation. Or the apprentice may be given permission to ask at least one or two people to leave the group with him when they are given the choice.

The second option is the reverse split. In this option the apprentice remains with the larger group, and the leader takes a few individuals to form a new group. The strength of this option is that the apprentice has a greater chance of success in leading a well-established group. Since the original leader has already proven his or her ability to lead, the smaller group should do well.

In order to facilitate this process, the group should be informed (as early as possible) that only a few members will leave to risk forming a new group. In order to avoid a mass exodus, you may limit the number of those leaving ("I'm going to be leaving this group and am looking for two other individuals to help me form a new group so that we can multiply our effectiveness and both groups can continue growing").

The third option is to have the apprentice begin the new group (no members from the old group). The apprentice who feels called to start a completely different group (in format, style, meeting night, content and membership) leaves the original group, recruits members and makes a completely fresh start.

The fourth option is that the leader begins a new group that does not include members from the old group. The original leader's ability to start a group has been established, so she has a better chance of success. In this option, the leader leaves the group, recruits new members and starts a brand-new group.

The fifth option is incubation—a leadership training course. Some churches have mandatory leadership training courses for leaders. These courses, often ranging in length from four to twelve weeks, complement apprentice training by formally training leaders. At the end of the course, the apprentices form their own groups.

Some churches use the training course to incubate groups. In an incubated group training, participants are allowed to be in groups during the course of the training, with the understanding that they will remain together when they are released. Thus each new group formed out of the training is "salted" with at least three or four leaders (allowing for several group splits before new leaders need to be trained).

Option six is turbo—every member forms a new group. The group sends *each individual* out to form and lead a separate small group. At some point, the original group will have changed its covenant in order to reflect its intention to be a leadership training group. The group will have discussed leadership issues and will have given each person the opportunity to lead meetings and be evaluated.

A final comment about apprenticing: The original leader is responsible for the apprentice until the apprentice is established and is working well under the church's supervision. The original leader should call the apprentice after group meetings to process, listen, pray and evaluate her performance.

Goodby to the Old Group and Hello to the New

Have you ever said goodby to a dear friend? Both of you feeling uncomfortable, shuffling your feet and not knowing what to do? Saying goodby is difficult for many people. Many prefer to move on quietly and thus avoid confronting feelings that termination might bring: abandonment, rejection, sadness or even anger.

But lack of closure leaves us feeling empty and even lost. We can put our feelings off for later (and they *will* surface again at some point) or we can address them now. Group termination exercises are meant to bring these feelings out in a healthy manner.

We terminate our group, first, to celebrate the past. Some time should be spent reminiscing about past events, situations, relationships and anything else that members recall. By celebrating the past, we consider the impact we have had on one another. Instead of obsessing about our loss—always a human tendency—we focus on the good.

We also terminate our group to direct our energy toward the future. A group that is multiplying has much to celebrate. The expanded possibilities of ministry are exciting! We should spend time talking about future challenges and committing our way to God.

There are a number of ways to terminate. Some groups choose the "crockpot" method, terminating over a period of months. Perhaps the original group multiplies and forms two groups, but the original group continues meeting monthly for fellowship, sharing and prayer. This method must be carefully balanced with the demands and dynamics of the new groups to avoid causing resentment among new members, who could feel left out.

A second method is the "oven bake" method. A group decides to multiply, so it devotes a series of meetings to reminiscing, planning, praying and crying together. Such groups may use a healthy termination resource like Dan Williams's *Starting (and Ending) a Small Group* (InterVarsity Press).

A final method is the "microwave" method. These groups are ready to move on and they want to celebrate. So they make their decision and then they have a party. That final event marks the termination of the old and the beginning of the new.

Third-Generation Groups?

In the early church, and more recently in countries like China, the gospel spread because of persecution. As violent rulers scattered the church, God used their oppression to create countless new groups. As Christians scattered and multiplied, Christianity spread rapidly.

Christians who are not experiencing persecution can create similar dynamics through apprenticing, inviting newcomers, dividing into groups of four, praying for an empty chair and more. It is an imperfect process. Some church leaders have noted that there are few second- and third-generation small groups in American churches, which means that few groups have birthed new groups.

But groups that do multiply are participating in God's plan to evangelize the world, and they are preparing their group structure to accommodate new believers. By God's power, more groups will take such risks, and they will enjoy God's blessing in the process. If your group prays, plans and disciplines itself well, it may take its place as one of the few groups in the Western world that birth second- and even third-generation groups.

5

Groups That
Serve the Church

Small groups can exert a powerfully positive impact on their churches. Chuck's group did.

Chuck is a quiet man who never served on leadership boards or in high-profile positions in his congregation. Consequently, when a small group leadership event was advertised, he wondered whether he had anything to offer. Putting aside his feelings, however, he attended the training. Following the event, he started a men's group with men from his congregation.

Group leadership challenged Chuck with situations he had never confronted before. With some coaching from other leaders, however, Chuck positively nurtured the men in his group. He was surprised to discover within himself, by God's gracious touch, a hitherto unknown reservoir of creativity and love.

Because men's lives were being transformed by God, other men wanted to join. Soon Chuck realized that one group was not enough. An apprentice was trained and another group was formed. Eventually yet another men's group was added. Chuck's ministry went largely unnoticed, perhaps because it happened so naturally.

A new dimension to his ministry began when a few men from several of the men's groups decided to meet for intercessory prayer on Saturday mornings. A visit to the sanctuary on one of those mornings would have revealed seven to twelve men, some sitting, some kneeling, some perhaps walking around, all in deep conversation with the Lord of the universe. After one such meeting, the men discussed an outreach retreat for the other men of the church. The retreat was a success. Soon another group formed. In the summer, a busload of men traveled to a large Promise Keepers event. Men formed Bible studies at work. They began to care more at home. And they served the church with more willingness and confidence.

All of this happened because a quiet man named Chuck felt a calling and responded in obedience.

Positive Power and Negative Power

Those who walk with God embrace the idea that God's power is greater than any power known to humanity. We derive comfort and assurance, as well as confidence, from Scriptures such as Matthew 28:18: "All authority in heaven and on earth has been given to me."

Small groups that embrace God's power bring energy and vitality to local congregations. They dream up new ideas. They create new ministries. They empower new leaders.

Unfortunately, not all small groups exert a positive influence, and not all small groups are attached to positive congregations. If church growth statistics are accurate, the majority of congregations have reached a membership plateau. Many churches, large and small, suffer from internal strife and discord. God's people and groups are prone to discouragement and disillusionment. Small groups can be sidetracked from God's power to human weakness, and when that happens they experience defeat.

A small group had been meeting at Cliff and Shirley's home for several years. Members had developed a deep bond of love. The group had grown by inviting both church members and non-Christians. Consequently, the group included a healthy mix of younger and older believers. All participants had experienced God's grace because of the small group.

The small group participated in a congregation from a mainline denomination. The church had a long history, dating its ministry back several generations to a single ethnic group that had originally settled the area. During the course of its history, the church had grown with the community and currently had a mix of peoples. Unfortunately, the church was experiencing something of a funk. Its dynamic ministry seemed to be a thing of the past. It was dying, and the pastor appeared willing to let nature take its course.

Members of Cliff and Shirley's group brought back stories of frustration as they tried to work in the church. Creative initiatives were quashed in committees; committee meetings were long and boring; nobody seemed to get involved in church activities; energetic members were frequently left "holding the bag."

The church environment began to have an impact on the small group. Cliff and Shirley became despondent. Other members slowly followed their lead. Eventually the group lost its energy, and it disbanded. The church continued to slide. And members of the now defunct small group embraced a scary principle: never bring new people and new believers from your group into the church.

The church that Cliff and Shirley attended took tremendous pride in its history. It celebrated its fiftieth and hundredth anniversaries with enthusiasm. Its pastor loved his position in the denomination. Its committees had been together for years and prided themselves in their stability and work. Its building, if somewhat worn, was proudly maintained.

But the church was dying, and not for lack of effort, location or people. It was dying because it had forgotten its heart.

Why Do We Exist?

It is easy for people to forget why they are doing what they do. Vacation Bible school may once have been conducted with missionary passion and heart. But what happens after three, ten or fifty years? People can forget its purpose and end up concentrating on "filling slots." As focus disappears, joy dissipates. We choose curriculum, find staff and prepare materials, and then for one or two (or even more) weeks we suffer our way through the project. In our church programming we do the same kinds of things with music, classes, small groups and special events.

Jesus made some key pronouncements that remind us of our purpose and challenge our reasons for existing. His Great Commandment is found in Matthew 22:37: " 'Love the Lord your God with all your heart and with all your soul and with all your mind.' This is the first and greatest commandment. And the second is like it: 'Love your neighbor as yourself.' All the Law and the Prophets hang on these two commandments." His New Commandment is found in John 13:34: "A new command I give you: Love one another. As I have loved you, so you must love one another. By this all men will know that you are my disciples, if you love one another." In John 17:23 Jesus prays the Great Prayer: "May they [all believers] be brought to complete unity to let the world know that you sent me and have loved them even as you have loved me." Giving them the Great Commission (Matthew 28:19), Jesus told his disciples to "go and make disciples of all nations, baptizing ['incorporating'] them in the name of the Father and of the Son and of the Holy Spirit."

In each of these key moments Jesus was providing overarching purpose statements for his believers. The redundancy serves to emphasize his heart. God's people will be his special community of faith, receiving God's love and sharing it with others. The small group that remembers this thrives. The small group that forgets it dies.

The Church of Our Dreams

Imagine that Cliff and Shirley had been participating in a vital, dynamic congregation that understood its purpose. New believers brought into their small group and loved would also be assimilated into the life of an encouraging congregation. They would be cheered on at every step of their spiritual, mental and emotional development. They could try and fail without disapproving glares and hurtful comments. They would not be expected to master all of the elements of doctrine and lifestyle immediately. They would be allowed to grow at their own (and the Spirit's) pace.

A church like that will grow. It will devise ministries that meet actual needs. It will creatively listen to the Spirit and allow itself to be molded, changed and shaped by God.

Yet even as we imagine this church, we realize how difficult it is to create. When Jesus told the parable of the wheat and the weeds, he served notice that nothing in this world, including our spiritual environment, will be free of problems. The bad always gets mixed in with the good. Where God is, Satan tends to follow.

The church of our dreams exists in heaven. That is the place where believers will exist in true unity. That is the place where we will forsake debates about hymns versus praise music and engage in the true, uninterrupted worship of our God. That is the place where our hearts will find their true rest.

Is there nothing we can do in the meantime? Of course there is. We can practice putting into effect the commands, prayers and commissions of Jesus Christ. If we are to accomplish this *through small groups*, we must concentrate on finding our place and service in the body of Christ.

The Church as a Series of Relationships

First, we must learn to perceive the church as a series of relationships, or cliques. The term *clique* has a negative connotation because most cliques are exclusive, consisting of a group of persons operating within the safety of exclusive relationships. Members seldom venture out of the clique to meet and engage other persons.

But cliques have positive sides too. In fact, we cannot survive without cliques. They provide safety. They offer a place to belong. They give acceptance. The reality is that most people have but a few deep friendships. Cliques acknowledge this reality, and Christian cliques offer *koinonia*. What separates Christian cliques from others is that they must connect us to the accepting, grace-giving love of Jesus Christ. Groups that know this love are more willing to reach out. They have compassion for those who hurt. They have energy to give.

And they influence the church in a positive manner. In Matthew 5, Jesus told his disciples to be both salt and light. Salt penetrates. It moves in and flavors everything around it. Light permeates. It boldly drives away darkness. Salt is subtle; light is invasive. We are to be both.

Cliff and Shirley's small group allowed the tables to be turned. An alive, spiritually focused group allowed an unhealthy church to destroy its growth.

But in Christ's kingdom, these dynamics change. The clique influences the church. It penetrates slowly as its members are taught to care, as they pray for and love all with whom they have contact. It flows through the church as its group love stands in stark contrast to what is happening in the congregation.

If Cliff and Shirley had been able to redirect the focus of their group from obsessing about structural change (over which they had no control) to concentrating on being one small piece of the body, they might have been able to make a difference. One at a time, relationships in the church would have deepened. Over time, other groupings would have noticed the dynamism of the one small group. I know of several congregations that have changed completely from the bottom up, without waiting for structural changes to occur or strategic decisions to be made. Instead, one group and then more formed. They lived out the Christian life in difficult circumstances, and the church changed.

The Church as the Body of Christ

Second, we must learn to use our small group's gift to build up the body of Christ. First Corinthians 12 (verses 7, 12 and 21) contains the most comprehensive statements in Scripture about spiritual gifts. Although this passage appears to be addressed to individuals, it can also speak to groups. It says that to each group the manifestation of the Spirit is given for the common good. The body is made up of many parts, not just one. The group cannot say to the body, "I don't need you!"

Small groups face the two temptations listed in 1 Corinthians 12. They are tempted to negate their place in the body of Christ, and they are tempted to remove themselves from the body of Christ (due to their inherent importance). Both attitudes are wrong.

Every group has a gift that it must bring to the body of Christ. Some churches use their small groups as ministry teams to build up the body of Christ—parking cars, ushering, working with young people, praying for specific items and so on.

Cliff and Shirley could have focused their group on meeting one positive need in the church (perhaps visiting shut-ins monthly or some other ministry based on the gifts and desires of group members). This one ministry would not guarantee systemic change in the congregation, it's true, nor would it renew the congregation's energy and desire. Yet as an act of simple obedience, the group's willingness to serve speaks volumes about God's work in the life of that one group. Such dynamics produce positive change in churches.

Where to Begin

There are a number of ways that dynamic groups can feed congregations. They can begin with the prayer of surrender. Many of us learn to pray by stating our case to God and then trying to convince God that our idea is correct. There is nothing necessarily wrong with such an approach, especially if we picture ourselves as children presenting requests to the Father.

However, change in your church begins with change in your life. As members of a particular congregation, you may want to distance yourselves from the church's apathy and dysfunction. Yet you are probably an unknowing participant in it.

Take Cliff and Shirley. Their tendency to be either enthusiastic change agents or people on their way out the door demonstrates an "all or nothing" approach that is probably common to their congregation. There is a very dysfunctional tendency here: using human means to fix something. When it doesn't get fixed, we quit in disgust. Let us thank God for God's legendary patience (Psalm 103)!

When Cliff and Shirley (and their group) surrender their desire to change the church and ask God to change *them*, God will be free to work. On several occasions Jesus told his disciples to (1) deny themselves (even their wishes and desires), (2) take up their cross (commit to something or someone even if it is difficult) and (3) follow him (possibly somewhere we don't want to go).

Turn the focus of prayer away from the church and onto the group. In the context of confession and surrender, ask God what he wants to do in and through the group (and, by extension, the church). When Jesus had finished commissioning his disciples, he told them to make disciples of all people (Matthew 28:18-20) and to wait (Acts 1).

Waiting on God requires patience and the ability to listen. Both can be in short supply in the church. I know a woman who wakes up every day and asks Jesus to lead her to the persons and ministry that he wants from her in that day. I know many more people who wake up and do what they did the day before. It is much harder to listen than to work.

For Cliff and Shirley's group, this step may mean reading a book by Henri Nouwen (for example, *The Way of the Heart*) and praying through its chapters. It may mean engaging in serious self-reflection so that the group is better able to see itself (and the church), so that it may better minister within itself (and the church).

Discuss ways that the group may minister specifically to the church. Through prayer the group will grow stronger in its community (and its ability to be salt to the congregation). Through service the group may become light to the congregation.

To guide your brainstorming, you may list each of the different groups and subgroups that exist within the church (perhaps by age). For example, one of your categories may consist of men and women seventy-five years and older.

Then consider how these groups may *not* be ministered to within the context of the church. For example, perhaps nobody is focusing prayer on the teen group. Or seniors over seventy-five may need help getting to clinics and doctors.

Finally, prayerfully consider which ministry you feel called to. Your ministry should be shared passionately by all in the group, should be realistic for the group to do (for example, you should not make rides to clinics and hospitals available if your members all commute to work during the day) and should solve a legitimate problem within the church.

Ways Your Small Group May Serve Your Congregation

1. Coordinate meals for new mothers
2. Offer nursery care and babysitting for special occasions
3. Provide rides for the elderly
4. Provide rides to doctor's appointments and hospitals
5. Straighten the sanctuary after services
6. Help fold bulletins and newsletters
7. Coordinate/help with the church telephone ministry, keeping in touch with shut-ins, absentee worshipers and all church members
8. Usher church services periodically (monthly?)
9. Greet at periodic services
10. Lead a monthly prayer service for the church
11. Send care packages to college students
12. Adopt several older members and visit them regularly
13. Adopt a grieving person and work through grief issues
14. Help park cars at worship services
15. Help shovel snow
16. Adopt a flower bed or other landscape feature for maintenance
17. Cut the grass monthly
18. Collect communion cups after communion services and wash them
19. Coordinate a church clean-up day
20. Coordinate a day to help the church clean its closets and storage spaces
21. Coordinate efforts to pray with people following services
22. Collect books for a church and/or small group lending library

---

Because group members are probably busy, your idea will need to be simple and reasonable. Starting an exciting ministry and then dropping it because no one has time to follow through offers a negative testimony. Make sure that you have the time and energy that the ministry requires.

The Power of One

People have a tendency to address symptoms and not causes. In our churches we complain about staffing, attendance, spirituality and apathy, four sources of constant pain and worry.

Jesus was not a complainer. He did not obsess about the political situation in Rome or the immorality of Herod's court. He did not argue the validity of certain taxes, where to build roads or why there was so much poverty and disobedience in the world.

Instead he demonstrates to us the "power of one." One person—

born in an obscure town and possessing neither money nor earthly power nor trappings of success—changed the world. He did it not by speaking earth into existence, as he did on creation day. He changed the world by living an obedient, faithful life as a servant. He died as our sacrifice for sin. And he rose again to completely defeat sin and death.

Starting with his life on earth and continuing into the present day, one person at a time has been changed by the one person who gave us our start. So it is with each small group. If we want to be agents of change, we need to understand our place relationally (as salt) and spiritually (as light) as we minister one person at a time, to the glory and honor of our God and Savior, Jesus Christ.

6

Groups That Support Mission

Why would small groups care about far-off missions?

Colleen's small group perceives itself as home base for the Sullivan family, missionaries to a far-off land. The Sullivans had been members of their church for years when God called them into missions. One of the small group members, a realtor, had offered to donate his commission from the sale of their home to speed up their move. Other members open up their homes to the Sullivans when they return from the field. One member cares for the Sullivans' car. Others send gifts and financial support. At every meeting the group prays and shares members' latest letters and e-mail messages from the Sullivans. The members laugh along with their friends' victories and cultural gaffes and weep along with their struggles and pain. Several members of the group intend to join the Sullivans as short-term missionaries.

If you were to ask the group why members support the Sullivans so enthusiastically, you would probably hear, "Because they are our friends, and whatever they do is an extension of our life and ministry together."

The Mission Enterprise

Imagine a world without missionaries.

That world existed until just a few centuries ago. The globe was essentially split into two halves: east (non-Christian) and west (Christian). God's people did not exhibit a restless desire to cross borders, cultures or language barriers with the gospel.

That began to change in the eighteenth century as long pent-up spirituality exploded, through the Holy Spirit, into acts of selflessness, courage and generosity never before envisioned. The nineteenth and twentieth centuries have witnessed the greatest mission thrust in all of church history. Christianity has experienced explosive growth throughout the world.

Never before in history have the non-Christian peoples of the world been so open to the claims of Christ. Missions, in all walks of life, are showing an unprecedented interest in the Christian faith. Animists in Africa, Hindus in India, Buddhists in Southeast Asia, Muslims in the Middle East are reading Christian literature, listening to gospel broadcasts, and enrolling in Bible correspondence courses in record numbers. Everywhere the Holy Spirit is at work, creating a hunger for the Bread of Life. And this quest for spiritual reality is not confined to the poor and the oppressed whose interest in religion might be suspect. The quest includes students in the universities, government personnel, military officers, professional and business people. The newer churches in the Third World, with few exceptions, are throbbing with vigor and vitality.[1]

Mission Resources and Biographies

Elliot, Jim. *The Journals of Jim Elliot*. Edited by Elisabeth Elliot. Old Tappan, N.J.: Revell, 1978.

Houghton, S. M., ed. *Five Pioneer Missionaries*. London: Banner of Truth, 1965.

Kyle, John F., comp. *Perspectives on the Unfinished Task*. Ventura, Calif.: Regal, 1984.

Muggeridge, Malcolm. *Something Beautiful for God: Mother Teresa of Calcutta*. New York: Ballantine, 1973.

Richardson, Don. *Peace Child*. Ventura, Calif.: Regal, 1974.

Stott, John R. W. *Christian Mission in the Modern World*. Downers Grove, Ill.: InterVarsity Press, 1975.

Taylor, Alice Hudson. *Rescued from the Dragon*. Basingstoke, U.K.: Marshalls Paperback, 1982.

Thornburg, John F. *David Brainerd: Pioneer Missionary to the American Indians*. Darlington, England: Evangelical Press, 1996.

Any discussion of world mission includes such issues as martyrdom, bravery, colonialism, the interchange between differing cultures and Spirit-driven global evangelism. Yet at the forefront of our minds is often the legacy of determined individuals who are passionately focused on winning the lost for Jesus Christ.

The Dark Side

Popular biographies of nineteenth- and twentieth-century missionary pioneers project images of rugged individualists carving Christ's kingdom out of a resistant world. We envision David Livingstone traversing "deep, dark Africa" alone. We picture Granny Brand, rejected by home mission boards because she was a woman, being carried from mountain to mountain in remote parts of India. We romanticize the courage of John Paton, missionary to cannibals in the South Pacific, and Adoniram Judson, first American missionary (to Burma). These favorite mission stories read like a modern-day Hebrews 11:

> Through faith [they] conquered kingdoms, administered justice, and gained what was promised; who shut the mouths of lions, quenched the fury of the flames, and escaped the edge of the sword; whose weakness was turned to strength; and who became powerful in battle and routed foreign armies. Women received back their dead, raised to life again. Others were tortured and refused to be released, so that they might gain a better resurrection. . . . They were stoned; they were sawed in two; they were put to death by the sword. They went about in sheepskins and goatskins, destitute, persecuted, mistreated—the world was not worthy of them. (Hebrews 11:33-35, 37-38)

Every act of bravery was accompanied by an act of sacrifice. Some missionaries left their children behind. Children who accompanied their parents to the mission field often experienced culture shock when they returned to their own people. Missionaries on the field suffered loneliness and depression. Churches would sometimes cut off their financial and prayer support when missionaries engaged in activities they did not approve of. The challenge of raising financial support left some missionaries burned out.

Many of these difficulties can be traced to the support network (or lack thereof) that missionaries built around themselves. Missionary Paul McKaughan says,

> As I began to get to know my fellow missionaries, I discovered the myth of the Lone Ranger was nothing more than that—a myth. Instead of always being victorious, missionaries were bruised and battered people who were hurting. I began to see that many times toward the end of their ministry, even the rugged individualists—those very strong personalities God had used in such a wonderful way to go out and start churches—had to leave the churches they had started because the people couldn't stand them. Personality quirks had arisen, or colleagues who had welcomed their leadership at first saw they were beginning to lose some of the forcefulness of their personality or leadership skills. There was no net to catch these men, and they were more or less put on a shelf. It has only been in the past few years that I have come to see the importance of the Church. Through working with a team of people, I began to see the necessity of the Body of Christ functioning together.[2]

Churches did nothing to discourage a "lone ranger" mentality in missionaries. The penchant that they shared with the rest of the Western world for results and victories could pressure mission workers to ignore personal issues and press on for the greater good. The church shares in the responsibility for burned-out missionaries and disillusioned missionary kids.

The church of Jesus Christ is awakening to mission issues. Christians are becoming more knowledgeable about missionaries' needs (as well as about the needs of those they serve) through short-term missions, conferences like InterVarsity's Urbana (in Illinois), a greater emphasis on indigenous mission (combined with a greater sensitivity to how Christianity interacts with other cultures) and missiology (the study of mission).

If mission is to continue and all unreached groups are to be evangelized, the church is going to have to assume a greater support role.

The Base Camp
The base camp for mission is the church. In the church people use their

spiritual gifts. In the church people practice their faith. In the church people learn about God's community. And out of the church go people who start other churches, all over the world.

In the context of community, and out of this context, mission must occur. While some people may flourish as lone-ranger servants, the vast majority need support. That support must come from the church.

Unfortunately, many churches elect a committee, which they then expect to fulfill *all* mission responsibilities. Committee members write letters, provide a "minute for mission" in church every now and then, determine support levels (and interview potential missionaries) and perhaps hold a mission conference to stimulate interest.

There is nothing wrong with the work of a mission committee *if* the larger church is involved in mission. The two scenarios that follow demonstrate the difference that a community orientation can make.

Scenario 1: Christ the King Church. Christ Church is located in the downtown area of a medium-sized town. It has existed for over a hundred years and has enthusiastically supported mission in recent decades. It devotes about 12 percent of its annual budget to mission (around $38,000), splitting the money between about twenty-five different organizations and individuals. People applying for support write a letter and receive an interview. If the committee votes to support them, they tend to be put in the budget every year. Each year there is a mission conference and several missionaries (some home, perhaps one or two foreign) make presentations that include lectures, slide shows and crafts.

Scenario 2: First Church. First Church has about five hundred members and is located in a suburban community. The congregation is active and has a strong interest in mission. It allocates about 20 percent of its budget to mission, or $45,000. It provides significant support to two separate mission families from the congregation and provides smaller amounts to another ten missions.

Of First Church's twenty small groups, about ten have adopted a mission to support. They offer prayer support, Christmas gifts, cards and letters. Several have held fundraisers for special needs. Each Easter all of the small groups gather clothing for the orphanage run by one of the mission families from their congregation.

Of these two scenarios, First Church has the stronger mission emphasis. Because the support for mission at First Church is decentralized, participation is greater and enthusiasm is higher. The result is that its mission families receive more consistent support and feel affirmed. This is the kind of mission support that a community-based model offers.

The Focus of Support

As you identify ways your group can get involved, you should concentrate on meeting real needs. Intentionally supporting missionaries involves doing research, listening and making careful choices. Nobody wants to waste effort on well-intentioned but unfocused giving. There are five areas you may want to consider as to consider supporting missionaries.

Prayer support. Mission organizations all over the globe are recognizing, and touting, the power of prayer. As the world shrinks into a single global village, Christian research is uncovering some interesting trends. One is the realization that the greater the prayer focus, the greater the harvest.

Persons from all traditions, from mainline to Pentecostal, fundamentalist to evangelical, recognize the importance of prayer. Some organizations may concentrate prayer against territorial spirits (the idea that certain demons rule certain geographic locations), while others pray for receptivity and a softening of a people's heart. But all prayer is needed.

Small groups that feel called to mission prayer should build time for prayer into their covenant. Each time they gather, at the appropriate time, they can pray for mission. Try to avoid scheduling this prayer time at the end of a meeting, where it might get bumped aside. After your initial group sharing and before your study is a good time slot.

Some groups may purchase *Operation World: A Handbook for World*

Intercession (by Patrick J. Johnstone) and pray for a different country or people group each time they meet. Other groups may adopt a mission family from their church. If they send for information, they will be added to mailing lists that continually update prayer requests. Still other groups may adopt an unreached people group, a country or a continent. Again, obtaining concrete information allows the group to pray for actual needs.

Groups that pray may want to consider purchasing *With Concerts of Prayer* by David Bryant (Regal Books) and hosting their own prayer concert. Other praying groups might help you to plan and host the event.

Concrete expressions of friendship. Depending on where they are located, mission families can feel isolated and alone. Some have no problem living in a strange culture and learning a different language and customs. Most, however, struggle with loneliness and frustration from time to time. Leaving behind everything that is familiar, as mission families must do, is difficult.

Receiving love gifts, letters and other expressions of care would make any missionary feel special. The possibilities of thoughtfulness are limited only by the creativity of your group.

If your group chooses to offer such expressions of friendship, it may "adopt" a special missionary family (or two). Correspondence with the family, sensitively worded, may help you discern ways that you can be most helpful. You may send Christmas presents (remember to mail them early), birthday presents and care packages. You may write to the missionaries themselves, and if they have children, the children of group members may want to write to them. Don't forget the Internet, which may allow cheap correspondence through e-mail. And if you get really creative, a long-distance phone call or even video conference will give your group an exciting evening!

Before you actually jump in, first make sure that your contact with the missionary family will not create trouble. Agents of authoritarian regimes may rifle through the family's mail. As a general rule, don't mention politics or world leaders in letters. Second, make sure that any packages you send are legal according to the rules of the country receiving them. Again, you don't want to get the family in trouble with customs agents or the local police.

Support a mission family. As the Western world begins to adopt a less assertive posture on the world stage, Westerners may tend to cocoon. This withdrawal will negatively affect mission support raised in the West.

Many mission groups are already experiencing fundraising difficulties. In mainline churches, for example, mission giving has dropped slowly (off and on) for thirty years. That trend is not showing signs of reversing itself anytime soon.

If your group is from a church that appears to have little interest in mission, you may choose to support a missionary financially. Just be sure that this giving is over and above your faithful support of the local church. A continuing witness in your local area (your church) is important to ensure the existence of potential mission support in the future.

A better alternative for groups from mission-active (or moderately active) congregations is to find tangible, perhaps periodic, ways to support a missionary's ministry. For example, a missionary might need five hundred Bibles. Your group could either donate the money or hold a fundraiser to generate help. Another missionary might need supplies for a local orphanage. Your group could collect clothes and baby supplies and then pay to ship them. The missionary you are supporting may know about ways to ship goods for less, so you should be sure to consult that person before actually mailing anything.

Perhaps the missionary you are supporting shares a need for money. Be aware that money can simply vanish in many countries, and sending it directly or wiring it to the missionary is unwise. Any money that you wish to send a missionary should be routed through the sponsoring mission organization.

Support a mission child. Many groups, families and individuals have supported orphan (and impoverished) children through organizations such as World Vision and Compassion International. They have found this to be a gratifying and concrete way to meet the spiritual, physical and emotional needs of children.

The care that you provide through this kind of organization includes at least one large meal per day, a set of clothes, an education and some loving attention. Most organizations will send you a picture of "your" child and will allow you to send correspondence and packages. You will receive periodic updates, letters from the child and pictures. Some individuals and groups have maintained a relationship with a child for many years.

Because of the expectations and needs of the children, you will want to make sure that your group is ready for such a commitment. Support can involve $30 per month. You don't want to leave one of your group members holding the bag if the group disbands or takes a few months off in the summer.

Some groups have found it helpful to save money for several months, building up an account and checking the commitment of the group. Then they contact the organization, fill out the forms and start sending their support.

Go! Any contribution that you make will be enhanced by sending a representative or a group of people to visit the missionaries. More on this in chapter seven.

Getting Started

If your group decides to support a missionary, how will you decide what option(s) is best? First, pray! Ask God to show you the choice that is best for your group.

Second, consider having a brainstorming session. You can invite a representative from the mission committee (or your pastor) to help you list possibilities. Begin by crossing off those that do not make sense for your group, and then consider assigning the remaining ones to individuals for research. One individual might send for information from Compassion. Another individual might correspond with several church missionaries to determine what help they need—and so forth.

Third, have everyone report their findings and then prayerfully choose your option. Make sure that you contact your church's leadership regarding the propriety of your decision. Then you can get started!

An Integrated Approach

Group mission involvement works best when your congregation takes an integrated approach to mission. As I write this, my congregation has been setting up a ministry to Romania for the past year. We have befriended missionaries and indigenous Christians. We have sent a team to Romania to do research, as well as an individual on several other occasions. We have met with several organizations that have ministries in Romania. We have decided to establish our own thrift shop (to teach business, management and ownership skills) and orphanage (supported by the thrift shop, an intentionally long-term, nurturing ministry, for some of the many orphan children of Romania).

When we actually set up the thrift shop, we will use our small groups to collect and box the hundreds of items that we must send (we are purchasing space in a truck trailer). Then, as the orphanage swings into gear, we will have dozens of ways for our groups to get involved—by sponsoring their own child, by collecting and mailing hygienic goods and toys, by praying for the ministry and more.

The Context of Community

Small groups provide a safe place for Christians and seekers to learn and grow. When groups support missionaries, they are expanding the boundaries of their community to embrace ministry opportunities they may never have considered. They are also building relational foundations from which missionaries are strengthened, nurtured and encouraged.

7

Groups That Go on Short-Term Mission

A small group had been meeting at the Griffith home for several years. The group, consisting of mixed couples and singles, had experienced some significant spiritual moments together. Members had shared, prayed and studied together and had grown into a deeply caring community.

During the past year, however, the group had reached a plateau. Although there was no overt tension or disagreement, morale was languishing. The reason behind this was difficult to pin down, but group members spent time discussing their situation.

At a meeting the group considered how it could find new life and energy. During a brainstorming session (with notes being written on newsprint) the group tried to identify new issues and activities members could participate in. After the possibilities were narrowed down, a number of outreach and evangelism ideas remained on the newsprint. Members began to discuss the possibilities.

One member began talking about a short-term mission project she had participated in a number of years before. Sharon raved about her experience: "It changed my life!"

Other members were skeptical and had questions. "What will we do with our children?" "How will we all be able to afford a trip?" "How can we expect our bosses to allow us time off so that we can all go at the same time?"

But Sharon persisted, and the group hesitantly gave her permission to research a short-term project and directed her to bring the results back to the group in a month. She did her homework. She contacted her pastor and mission committee for missionaries who lived in a nearby country, allowing for lower-cost plane tickets. She wrote letters to missionaries, inviting their ideas on what the group could do, how much a project would cost, where they would stay and what they would eat. She summarized all their ideas and put together a trip prospectus for a project in the Dominican Republic.

Her proposal included how the group would prepare for the trip; how much the trip would cost (with breakdowns); how members might raise some of the money; where they would go; what they would do; what they would eat, drink and wear; and what the benefits would be. Her group was so impressed that members agreed to the trip.

All ten group members participated in team building and crosscultural sensitivity training, and eight members went on a two-week trip to the Dominican Republic. They participated in several small construction projects; they brought clothes, food and toys to an orphanage; they helped serve in several outreach ministries of a local church and even got to spend a day at a beach near the end of their trip.

The trip changed the dynamics of their group. Upon their return, the group felt called by God to pursue . . .

The possibilities are endless.

Why Short-Term Mission?

In the past thirty years short-term mission involvement has increased significantly. Churches and parachurch ministries are beginning to see that there are benefits to be gained in removing groups from the comfort zone of their particular culture and bringing them as a community into a new culture.

In a short-term mission project, persons who don't necessarily have a long-term crosscultural call to mission take the opportunity to serve. Short-term mission projects can take place in rural communities and inner cities. They can also lead people to another country or another continent. Short-term mission takes place wherever a need exists and a group feels called to respond.

Short-term mission is not for everybody. Persons with deep emotional disorders, low spiritual commitment or significant health problems will want to consider carefully whether or not to participate. (I once took a young man with a serious brain tumor to a rural mission project, and he had the time of his life.) In addition, short-term mission usually costs a significant amount of money, which often limits participation to individuals who have access to adequate financial resources.

Yet short-term mission captures the interest of a large cross-section of persons—young and old, rich and poor, spiritually mature and baby Christian. Almost everyone can enjoy the lessons learned in a short-term project. There are many benefits in a short-term mission project.

First benefit: risk. People who participate in mission are taking a risk, and risk involves faith. In a mission project risk may involve raising or spending the money necessary to go. It may involve traveling to a strange place. It may involve telling people about Jesus for the first time. And more.

When Christians put themselves in a position of risk, growth occurs. I have seen this dynamic in my own experience with mission, and I have observed it in others who have served. My call to ministry was influenced by short-term mission.

Second benefit: community. People get to experience community on a short-term mission project. The best way to get to know people is to live in community with them. In community we see the best and worst of one another. It is virtually impossible to maintain a "front" for two weeks, twenty-four hours a day. At some point makeup smudges, clothes get rumpled, hair becomes disheveled, tempers flare. When we let down our guard, we can experience authentic community, often for the first time.

I recall taking a group of young people to Haiti to work in an orphanage for two weeks. When the two weeks were over, it was time to get back on the plane and fly home.

But several young people resisted leaving. And all of the young people expressed regret at leaving.

Why did they want to stay? How could they be ready to turn their backs on their families and the comfortable American way of life? Were they really prepared to embrace a different climate, culture, language and living situation?

I believe they were ready to stay because they felt safe in community (a community, by the way, that included some wonderful Haitian Christians). We connected deeply with one another, and from that foundation we felt like we could make a difference. Such community is rare in everyday life. Of those who experience it, many want to hang on to it.

Third benefit: interaction. So far we have discussed the benefits of short-term mission from the perspective of those who participate. Some might think we are succumbing to me-generation thinking (tell me what I'll get out of it and then I'll decide to go). But the reality is that the greatest potential benefit from short-term mission accrues to the group that goes and to the church that welcomes them back.

Hosting short-term groups can be a significant source of stress to the missionaries who benefit from their help. And although the local persons receiving help may be touched in some way, long-term change usually involves a deeper commitment than short-term missionaries can offer.

So how can you benefit the place you visit and the people you meet? Think of your ministry as seed sowing. Share your love freely and openly, being a model of Christian faithfulness. Give as you are able, keeping in mind the needs (and not just wants) of those you are serving. When you leave, perhaps in the mind of one person you would never imagine, a seed will have been planted. That person will have a memory that he or she cannot shake. God will use that idea to create a yearning. Ultimately it is not what you can give that matters. It is only what God can give. Although we serve prayerfully, we will never know the benefits. But God will.

There are some don'ts. Don't try to change the world in two weeks. Don't push outside the limits of short-term mission. Don't pretend that you are making lifelong friendships when in fact you are leaving shortly. Don't measure results according to your ego.

Fourth benefit: long-term change. A final benefit from short-term mission is realized by your congregation when you return. For the group, it may involve a renewed commitment to evangelism and outreach. For the church, it may include more energy for its various ministries. And for individuals, it may lead to some interesting priority adjustments.

I know a family that has participated in short-term mission. Although family members do not feel called to long-term mission, two of the children have altered their career plans to become involved in helping people. Who knows how many others have experienced similar change?

What Are the Dangers of Short-Term Mission?

Despite the many benefits involved in short-term mission, there are some dangers. The first danger involves the individual and team dynamics of short-term mission groups. One mission team that traveled to another culture came back in disarray, fighting one another. Another mission trip for high-school students from various congregations that I participated in was a disaster. Some students from another church sneaked out at night and engaged in inappropriate activities. In each case the individual and group dynamics did not work well.

The second danger involves lack of sensitivity to the receiving culture. Westerners (most notably Americans) have a bad reputation for breaking cultural rules and possessing obnoxious attitudes—for example, an attitude that communicates, "Do you know who you're dealing with? We're Americans!"

Some of the potential cultural dangers touch on dress, personal behavior and sexuality issues. For example, it may be inappropriate for a man on your team to speak to a woman from the local culture. A number of years ago I took a team to Jamaica. Unlike our vacationing American counterparts, we wore sleeved shirts, long skirts and long pants. Many of our participants had to visit the Salvation Army to find clothes for the trip!

A third danger involves successful projects. Participants in a successful trip may feel exhilarated and may be tempted to go back to the same location the next year with far more participants and a developing expectation for similar results. Some people will end up living for the exhilaration, as many individuals do in regard to retreats. The result is that some churches end up sending people on trips, but little outreach is done around the church. To address these temptations, some churches vary project locations from year to year. Others form long-term partnerships with a particular people and location, drawing attention away from the experience and toward cultivating long-term relationships.

A fourth danger lies in romanticizing the people you are serving. I did this myself when I returned from Poland or Haiti and exclaimed, "Unlike Americans, those people are *real* Christians!"

In reality, those Christians possessed qualities such as simple faith in God's provision, which I needed to possess more of. But they also needed God's redemptive touch through Jesus Christ. We must be careful to see with Christ's eyes, not the eyes of our expectations, hopes and dreams. In this way, our perceptions will be less starry-eyed and more realistic.

A final danger involves the mission organizations you work with. It is a sad fact of life that some missions and organizations are scams. The money you give such organizations may never be applied to the purpose for which you gave it.

One short-term mission group I worked with researched its project thoroughly, but it nevertheless fell through just as we arrived. Our host missionary quickly located another project, and we got to work. On the last day of the project, our host missionary informed us that we had been serving a cult group. We had to tell our participants that they were allowed no further contact with those they had served in the project. We were heartbroken.

On an inner-city project, we helped renovate the inside of a home for a homeless ministry. A few months later a group member stopped by the home, which turned out to belong to a family member of the missionary. We felt that we had wasted our time and money.

You can minimize your risk of being scammed or defrauded by checking with denominational boards, local missionaries and fiscal accountability agencies.

Where Do We Begin?

Before embarking on a short-term mission, you must prepare well in three areas: (1) project logistics, (2) personalities of host missionaries and (3) team building.

Project logistics. I have found it helpful to either make a preliminary trip myself or have someone else travel to set up the project. Especially if you are traveling to a different country, it is good to check out the landscape in advance. Where will you be staying? What is required for housing reservations? How will you address transportation, customs, airports, meals, fundraising and building materials? Where will you be working? How safe is the area? How should you protect one another? Where will you keep money? How will you handle such money issues as exchange rates?

Before I lead a group on a project, I brainstorm every possible question I can think to ask. My planning then involves working backward to answer each question, creating in the process a trip prospectus and team workbook.

Personalities of host missionaries. It is helpful to gain some knowledge of those on site who will be helping you set up the project. For example, a missionary may have volunteered to help you with the project. She may have agreed to handle housing, meals, projects and materials from her end. You agree with her on a price and dates. But when you arrive at the airport, she is not there. Eventually a friend of hers arrives and you are ferried to your location (several trips required), only to discover that there are not enough beds and the food has not been purchased. When you ask her where you will serve tomorrow, she shrugs her shoulders and says that you'll decide that tomorrow!

Planning Checklist for Short-Term Mission Project

☐ Sift through possibilities, develop short list of projects
☐ Prayerfully choose a project that is financially, logistically, and spiritually realistic
☐ Create a trip prospectus/application that
    explores travel, housing, meal, and safety issues
    addresses language, project and other logistics issues
    creates expectations for the trip in terms of age, emotional stability and
      spiritual maturity
    lays forth cost, budget and fundraising issues
☐ Get all necessary approvals from church leadership
☐ Check on insurance liability issues
☐ Hold first meeting for information
☐ Set deadline for applications
☐ Finalize planning for travel, housing, meal, project
☐ Participate in team building (monthly? weekend retreat? weekly?):
    trust-building exercises
    communication exercises
    theological/biblical basis for mission
    language and crosscultural issues
    rules and expectations
☐ Insert spiritual growth emphasis into project (worship, sharing, teaching, prayer, debriefing times?)
☐ Plan debriefing exercise for end of project
☐ Share project's blessings and challenges at a special worship service/Sunday school class
☐ Evaluate project's effectiveness

In many Third and Fourth World cultures, such an approach to life is the norm. But a group that has raised money and expectations may want more. You need to communicate carefully on a regular basis with the missionary, asking specific questions so that you can gauge what you will find upon arrival.

Team building. Every group preparing for a mission project should spend at least six hours together (or better yet, two hours per week over the course of several months) discussing details, learning about the culture and building trust. The details and cultural issues come from the trip planning. The team building can be accomplished by breaking into groups of four and using problem-solving ideas from youth ministry resource books.

The Project

Participating in a short-term mission project is an adventure. Yet adventures can be spoiled by complaining and backstabbing. To avoid such problems, I emphasize two rules: (1) you may not complain about anything for the duration of the trip and (2) if you have a problem with somebody, either you tell that person or you keep quiet about the problem.

On one project an adult was bitten by a centipede on the first night of the trip, just as we were all preparing to lie down on cement floors (our beds for the next two weeks!). Later on, we had to bite our lips as ants trekked across our faces every night. Our situation gave rise to numerous jokes—a much more positive form of complaining.

Eating different food, having little freedom, having to wash hands repeatedly, and more, is difficult. Yet if we are to serve, we will find the humor in these circumstances and set aside our desire for comfort.

Mission projects are fun when people face adversity with a smile. The key word for dealing with life's difficulties on a project is *flexibility*. Flexibility demands that we bend and not break when we are dirty and smelly. Flexibility demands that we smile patiently while waiting for a 9 o'clock service to begin sometime around 10:30 (and end around 5:00 p.m.). Flexibility demands that we yield to one another when hot water runs out or that we work when we are tired. Flexibility demands that we pray for those we serve and that we listen when God asks us to include and empower them.

Group Process

Next to flexibility, group process helps to ensure a project's success. Every mission project should include daily time for both individual and group reflection. The morning may begin with individual reflection, followed by job assignments, explanations and a time of prayer.

Group reflection is often held in the evening, perhaps in the context of teaching or worship. You should set aside leisurely time for persons to share what they experienced, felt and learned during the day. This can be accomplished in smaller groups. The larger group may then address questions, concerns, joys and challenges.

Groups that skip process time will probably experience a diminished result. People tend to learn more when they can talk while they are learning. Groups tend to perform better when they can build community while they are serving. And individuals tend to be more creative when they are being heard and valued.

After the Project

Near the end of any project I coordinate, we usually try to take a day or two and have some fun. We might take a trip to the beach or stay at a nice motel for an evening (complete with hot running water). We do this partly to indulge ourselves but also to provide a relaxing environment that helps us create separation from the project. It also allows us prepare to reenter our everyday world.

In this time of processing, team building is still a key issue. We share, listen, pray, cry, worship and break bread (take communion) together. We hug, process our feelings and begin looking to the future. We discuss what the anticipated long-term change from this event may be. And we admit together that those back home who did not participate may never quite understand the power of the feelings we have.

When the group returns, it shares its story with the congregation, perhaps during the morning worship service or at an evening meeting. Be careful to avoid rambling stories, inside jokes and embarrassingly long slide shows that detail every moment of the trip.

Long-Term Change

Money spent on short-term mission is an investment in the potential for long-term change that results from the project. Some of the change is impossible to calculate. For example, God's call to ministry came to me when I was serving on my first project. Who could have planned that?

But some change is possible to calculate. One possible goal of short-term mission is to expose your congregation to mission, with the result that some may choose to become missionaries. This change becomes obvious over time.

A second outcome is that more congregation members become interested in future trips. If you sent one team with five people this year, don't be surprised when twenty people want to go next year and when a second team is added the year after that.

A third outcome involves attitudes, focus and action. A mission attitude creates an outreach focus, which leads to service. Churches that want to capitalize on short-term mission possibilities should educate returning individuals and groups on service evangelism, local mission and outreach possibilities.

8

Groups That Evangelize

The Wednesday-evening Bible study group had been together for about five years when it considered the subject of evangelism. Since the group was made up of mature believers, it understood that a new direction was necessary.

One member attended a small group conference and brought back a resource on small group evangelism. Group members eagerly embraced the idea of evangelism. They bought copies of the book, studied it together and discussed ways to implement what they learned. They decided to do evangelistic small group ministry.

The most difficult choice for them involved their existing group. They admitted the difficulty of disbanding their beloved group, yet they understood that in an evangelistic group seekers need to outnumber Christians.

After much prayer and discussion, they decided to split the group evenly into three evangelistic groups. They agreed that their current group would continue to meet monthly for fellowship, sharing and prayer.

The groups reformed and invited friends. One group thrived as non-Christians were led to Christ and were brought sensitively into the church. The second group experienced some success, as several seekers came to faith and a new group was formed. The third group did not fare as well. Repeated invitations to seekers were turned down, and the group never got off the ground. Frustrated both at their failure and at the loss of their group, members eventually assimilated into the second group.

The question is, Does this scenario represent a success or a failure?

Attack!

There are two ways to invade another country. One is to mass your forces on its border and then attack. This "attack from the border" approach is how, for example, Iraq invaded Kuwait in 1990.

A second invasion technique is to infiltrate a country's cultural and political systems slowly. This "attack subtly from within" approach is best symbolized by the covert operations employed by organizations like the C.I.A. and the old K.G.B.

Both techniques are useful to Christians trying to reach the souls of men and women with the gospel of Jesus Christ. The "attack from the border" approach has been used for several centuries by missionaries who "invade" other countries and cultures with the gospel. The "attack subtly from within" method is illustrated in efforts to evangelize college students from closed countries who are studying in this country, who may then take the gospel back to their people.

Small group evangelistic outreach can make use of both methods. The "attack from the border" approach includes evangelistic small groups and outreach events (the subject of this chapter). The "attack subtly from within" method is best illustrated in emphasis on small group sensitivity, care and outreach.

So What's the Difference?

What is the difference between small group evangelism and evangelistic small groups? Both use the small group format to share the good news of Jesus Christ. Both attempt to win people to Christ in a seeker-friendly environment. Both use a relational style of ministry that groups are known for. And both have a built-in follow-up procedure.

The differences are a function of intent and structure. The intent of an evangelistic small group is purely evangelistic. Non-Christians should outnumber Christians. Success depends on the number of seekers who come. The structure of an evangelistic small group tilts, therefore, toward an evangelistic component in every aspect of group life. Since non-Christians should outnumber Christians, prayer and sharing are simplified. Study questions, which may be simplified in small group evangelism, are even more simple and straightforward. They are oriented toward encouraging people to question whether or not Jesus is right for them.

Who Does Evangelistic Small Group Ministry?

Of all the ideas presented in this resource, evangelistic small group ministry is perhaps the most risky.

> When you launch an evangelistic home Bible study, you cross enemy lines. You have a specific purpose, to communicate the love of Jesus Christ in a way that others will be drawn to him as Savior and Lord. Of course, as soon as people become Christians, you add a second dimension to your study, to help them grow and communicate the love of God to others. In this spiritual battle, Satan will not give up his territory easily.[1]

Evangelistic small group ministry shares dynamics with new church development. Risk is high. A committed core of workers is called for. Christians must be creative and must be good listeners. Believers must be bold.

Unfortunately, many Christians back away from the challenges of evangelistic small group ministry. "Can't we do something safer?" they ask. But where would *we* be if early Christians had similarly backed away? In Acts 4, facing the threat of persecution, the Christians (many of them baby Christians) prayed not for safety but for boldness (Acts 4:29). Such courage is called for in the post-Christian world in which we live.

Were the group evangelistic efforts described at the beginning of the chapter a success or a failure? Releasing mature believers to share their faith in a high-risk venture is difficult, and one group did suffer somewhat for its efforts. But as a result of the effort new believers were nurtured into the faith and a new group was formed. That is success.

Evangelistic small group ministry attracts a wide range of Christians, including mature and baby Christians, bold personalities and quiet listeners, some who are well versed in Scripture and some who are just "scratching the surface." What all these people have in common is a shared conviction that God is calling them to outreach and a shared accountability that they are in this together. Such groups become a mighty force in the hands of God!

Evangelistic small group ministry takes three forms. First, preevangelistic groups attempt to meet felt needs in the community, with the goal of identifying some who want a Christian group experience. Second, evangelistic small groups form for the express purpose of winning friends, colleagues, neighbors and family to Christ. Third, penetrative evangelistic small groups cross cultural boundaries to identify and win unknown persons to Christ.

Preevangelistic Small Groups

One often untapped means of evangelism is the preevangelistic small group. These are groups that form to meet a specific community need. For example, Carol was a concerned mother who had been witnessing deterioration in the local schools for years. She began praying with a group of mothers, and one day they brainstormed ways that they could (1) make the schools a safer place, (2) equip parents to listen to and discipline their children and (3) provide a witness through their church to seekers.

The group approached the principal and then the school board with an idea for a family fair. The family fair would begin with a fun, creative all-school assembly for the children. Immediately after school and into the evening, a carnival atmosphere would provide wholesome games for families; outdoor assemblies involving community building, trust-building exercises and panel discussions; tables run by local family-building organizations to promote their services and the opportunity to sign up for six-week parent support groups (perhaps led by members of Carol's church or by local parenting experts).

A thousand people participated in the fair, and fifty signed up for groups. They formed seven groups and began meeting. For six weeks a dynamic, interactive support environment ("salted" by local Christian parents who were also learning) encouraged stressed-out parents to begin making changes for the better. At the end of six weeks, the groups disbanded. Then another option for a smaller pool of persons was proposed: a more in-depth group experience to be led by church members. In fact, Carol's group willingly disbanded in order to offer several meeting options.

Of the fifty community members who signed up for groups, about fifteen seekers signed on for a deeper group experience. Combined with the original members of the Christian groups, they formed four groups that examined parenting issues from a faith perspective.

Many groups reading this resource might want to put on the brakes at this point. This may sound like a bit much for individual small groups!

Of course, your plans need not be so elaborate. To simplify, you might choose a support group resource and then advertise your group and invite friends to participate. At the end of the unit, you may disband and invite those still interested to participate in a more faith-oriented support series.

Consider the benefits of such an approach. When you identify and meet a felt community need, the church begins to take a larger role in society. The church begins to be seen asserting its creativity and intelligence in meeting the complex needs of our day. As people begin to identify emotionally with the church, they become more open to the person and work of Jesus Christ.

If your group is interested in preevangelistic outreach, there are several steps you may take: (1) offer your group to God through prayer; (2) brainstorm community needs; (3) identify the need that most interests your group *and* for which you have either some group expertise or an awareness of available resources; (4) contact your church leaders and ask them to help you think through your ideas and locate helpful resources; (5) partner with other small groups; (6) create a time line and delegate responsibilities to group members; (7) consider the impact such decisions will have on your small group (should you disband entirely? disband for a period of time? continue to meet monthly? stay together and do this ministry as an outgrowth of your small group?); (8) hold a seminar or a time-bound small group (remember, don't let Christians outnumber seekers!); (9) invite those interested in a deeper experience to join more faith-oriented groups.

Unfortunately, there are not a lot of printed resources on this approach, so you may have to chart your own path as you go along. Do make sure that you communicate clearly. Do not attempt to manipulate or cover up your purposes. In the seminar and early group experience, words like *faith* and *morality* will resonate with seekers and will prepare them for Jesus Christ when he is introduced at a later time.

Evangelistic Small Groups

Evangelistic small groups are formed for one purpose: to evangelize friends, family and neighbors (as opposed to crosscultural evangelistic small groups). They function best in a seeker atmosphere in which non-Christians outnumber Christians.

There are relatively few evangelistic small groups, owing probably to spiritual lethargy. Evangelistic small groups are a powerful means of reaching others with the gospel of Jesus Christ.

> One of the most appealing advantages of small groups is that they can be adapted to the needs and inclinations of almost any group of people. You can reach young married couples through them, retired senior citizens, homemakers, university students, musicians, teenagers. The content, style, environment and leadership will be quite different from social group to social group—but the dynamic within the group will be the same; and so will the potential for sharing the gospel.[2]

Evangelistic small groups are unique. They welcome any and all seekers. Their meeting time is generally relaxed, relational and open. Seekers are invited to ask questions. There is no knowledge or godliness requirement. Such groups take on many personalities and emphases, always within a seeker framework.

Checklist for Starting an Evangelistic Small Group (adapted from Bob and Betty Jacks, *Your Home, a Lighthouse*, NavPress)

1. Form a team—one couple to lead the study, two couples to host the event.
2. Develop a list and prepare to invite two to three times more persons than the home can accommodate.
3. Send a card or a note.
4. Follow up with a personal invitation.
5. Use a study that is both biblical and practical.
6. Go all out to make those attending feel at home:
   pay attention to room layout, conversation, interruptions
   provide the same Bible translation for each person (preferably easy to understand)
   be time-sensitive
   do not try to change people; just love them
   avoid the appearance of a being in a clique with other members of the team

---

Lay leaders Bob and Betty Jacks began their evangelistic study efforts with another Christian couple and about twenty-five friends and acquaintances. "Out of that original study, over a ten-year period, some 25 groups were born. There were study groups at work, in people's neighborhoods, in schools, and couples', women's and men's studies. The outreach grew to where, at one time, there were about 400 people a month who were hearing the claims of Christ who otherwise may never have been touched with the gospel."[3]

Urban pastor Peter Scazzero documents his early experience in small group evangelism. If his friends would come to a Bible study, he would then go with them to the local bar (for a soft drink). He began the group with twenty individuals. "In three weeks the Bible study died. . . . Nevertheless, I knew I was on to something. A close look at the New Testament reveals that one of the reasons the gospel spread so rapidly was because new Christians witnessed powerfully to their friends, relatives, neighbors and coworkers."[4] From this experience, Peter and his wife went on to start seeker groups and founded the fast-growing New Life Fellowship in New York City.

We can extract several key points in regard to evangelistic small groups from the experiences described by Bob and Betty Jacks and Peter Scazzero.

1. Evangelistic small groups live and breathe prayer. Bob and Betty Jacks credit their success to prayer.

2. Participants are not afraid to fail. You will need to invite many individuals (perhaps seven invitations for each person who responds) in order to form a group of seekers. Some may consider a low response rate a sign of failure. Others, however, see each gathering of people, no matter how small, as an opportunity to share Jesus.

3. The groups are sensitive to the needs of seekers. They provide a safe physical, emotional and spiritual environment. High-minded Christians who have all the answers are not invited.

4. They openly focus on Jesus Christ. While some may be tempted to leave the name of Jesus out of invitations, others believe that interest in that name is the ultimate drawing card. Many people would love the opportunity to study the claims of Christ in a casual group setting that allows them to draw their own conclusions (with help from the Spirit).

5. Healthy evangelistic groups partner with the local church in nurturing new believers and providing them with an opportunity for worship and community so that they can grow as ministers and servants of Jesus Christ.

6. Most individuals and groups are willing to sacrifice their comfort (and group experiences) in order to do ministry. Thus they may consider disbanding an original group in order to concentrate on evangelism.

Crosscultural Evangelistic Small Groups

Bart participated one summer in a small group that met at a local park (or in his home in case of rain). The group sat on blankets and did Bible study together. One evening, he pointed out a popular bar that was across the street. Group members had never been in the bar.

His heart sensitized by God's prompting, Bart encouraged the group to pray for the people in the bar. In the weeks that followed, group members began to recognize the faces and automobiles of bar regulars. They identified a compassionate affinity with folks who, lacking a small group experience like their own, met together perhaps daily over drinks. The only difference was that they didn't meet to talk about Jesus.

Several of the group members began making plans to go into the bar after their group meetings so that they could get to know some of the patrons. They implemented their plan and began to develop relationships with interested and sometimes lonely individuals. Eventually, their ministry flourished and they began to speak more boldly about God. A group materialized, and discussion at one table in the bar became spiritual.

This is an example of a crosscultural small group. Christians have used penetrative small groups to reach high-school and college students, temporary residents from other cultures, members of other cultures within their communities, truck drivers at truck stops and many others. The crosscultural small group is high-risk and requires special crosscultural (gender, age and demographic) sensitivities.

Groups doing such penetration need to address certain risks. First, they must understand how to speak to people who use perhaps different language and thought structures (for example, mechanics have a unique way of thinking and interacting). Second, they must discuss some of the temptations they may face. For example, alcoholics should generally stay away from bar ministries; men and women should understand healthy sexual and emotional boundaries, as well as their own sexuality, in higher-risk situations, since higher-risk situations generally provide greater temptation; and all group members should be able to identify their personal power issues. Third, they are willing to stand out in a new culture. People who do the best crosscultural ministry do not pretend to be something they are not. Instead they focus on their strengths, most notably their ability to be effective listeners and compassionate servants. Fourth, they must know how to wait for the appropriate moment to address faith issues.

If Toys Can Do It . . .

In the movie *Toy Story* the two toy heroes Buzz and Woody are taken against their will into the home of the evil neighbor boy Sid. Sid has a horrible habit of destroying toys or marring them so badly that they become distorted shells of their original forms.

Buzz and Woody are scared and then repulsed by the toys in Sid's room. As they get used to the environment, they give up their fear and merely ignore the toys. Finally, when the evil boy is about to blow up Buzz, Woody turns to the toys to help him save his friend. The toys band together, scare the meanness out of the boy and save Buzz.

In this movie Buzz and Woody engage in many evangelistic activities. They confront their own fears, build bridges and communicate. Finally they bring "salvation" and freedom from a common enemy.

What will it take to move the church of Jesus Christ (especially the church in the Western world) beyond the safety of its networked relationships and secure buildings into the world, where the need (and the harvest) is great?

9

Groups That Serve the Community

Every year there is a county fair in our town.

A county fair is a big deal for a small town. Local businesses, entrepreneurs, recreational vehicle dealers and a host of different groups gather together to peddle their wares and their messages. Churches and civic organizations purchase booth space to make money on everything from funnel cakes to crafts. Some organizations make a great deal of money at the fair.

One evening an evangelism team from our congregation was mulling over creative ideas for outreach. The subject of the fair entered the conversation.

We had never had a booth at the fair. Our church is new, and the fair tends to be dominated by old-timers in the local establishment. But this particular evening we had an idea. What if we built a booth in the shape of a church and gave things away instead of selling them? This idea for the fair was consistent with the bridge-building theme we had been developing as a congregation: as bridge builders we are to build loving bridges to our culture as an act of witness to our faith.

We honed our county fair idea in further brainstorming sessions. Then we moved into action. One group constructed a beautiful booth.

Another group worked with the leaders of the fair to obtain space. Still another developed craft and activity ideas to last the six days of the fair. As each idea was produced, it was given to another working team to develop. By the time the fair rolled around, we had plans for children's face painting, cupcake decorating and family Polaroid photos using professionally created backdrops (among others). During the fair we contacted thousands of people and handed out thousands of gifts.

Our "free" booth was a novelty at the fair. The booth next to us sold a variety of brushes and industrial goods. Each day as we rotated small groups of volunteers in our booth, the folks at the brush booth would amble over and talk. The people working our booth were shocked to hear our neighbors inviting all who would listen to come to *our* booth! We had an opportunity to share Jesus in a nonthreatening way in a fun-filled place. We had a great time.

Service Evangelism

Our county fair experience is an example of service evangelism. Service evangelism is outreach that is service centered. The community of faith leaves the security of church buildings for downtown streets, community centers, shopping malls, bars, county fairs or any other place where people gather. Christians participating in service evangelism enjoy the security of being part of a group (preferably a small group) and they are able to serve the needs of people who would not necessarily enter a church. Everybody benefits from the informal, relaxed, nonthreatening environment in which all kinds of conversation and evangelism can take place.

Service evangelism is not a new idea. The early church performed service evangelism when Christians ministered in the concrete and countless ways described in the pages of the New Testament. A Christian who ministers a "cup of cold water" to a person in need is performing service for the kingdom of Christ.

Service evangelism made a splash with the publication of Steve Sjogren's book *Conspiracy of Kindness*. I started reading Steve's book a few moments before I left for a denominational meeting. Intrigued by its first few pages, I grabbed it as I ran out the door.

I had some time left before the meeting started, so I stopped in at a donut shop, purchased a cup of decaffeinated coffee and continued reading the book. By the end of the meeting, I had finished the book (although I no doubt missed some life-changing debates). By the following weekend, I had purchased about a hundred copies of the book and made them available to my congregation. I even wrote a six-week small group study guide for group discussion.

This book is one that most, if not all, small groups can study. It is easy to read and full of stories. And it challenges the church to make an impact on the community.

What Good Does Service Evangelism Accomplish?

Results-oriented persons might question our church's county fair experience (and *all* service evangelism). What results did we achieve? How many new people did we bring into the church?

As far as we know, not one person attended our church as a result of our presence at the fair (although our friends at the brush booth predicted that many would come). Does this mean that the experience was a waste of time? I think not. There are several ways of analyzing the results of service evangelism.

Service evangelism offers Christians a tangible way of doing evangelism (and of being trained in evangelism). Becky Manley Pippert wisely notes that "Christians and non-Christians have one thing in common: they both hate evangelism."[1]

Evangelism is a "big league" kind of activity. Very few people can lead others to Christ naturally and effectively (perhaps excepting those who possess the spiritual gift of evangelism). Some studies show that fewer than 10 percent of Christians ever lead another person to Christ. Yet there is a "minor league" of witnessing in which Christians can supply words, actions and situations in a healthy learning environment. Service evangelism is such a school.

Ask a representative group of Christians how they feel about their witness in the world, and chances are you will get lots of "would, could and should" language. Then ask a similar group of Christians how they feel about their witness in the world after a service evangelism event. You will get lots of "did, learned and grew" language.

Service evangelism offers interactions with non-Christians that may bear fruit years later. Service evangelism communicates something about Christians that we are compelled by God's love to show: that God's gifts are "no strings attached."[2]

A results orientation can have a negative impact on evangelism. Once I was on a Caribbean island when a famous evangelist pulled up in a huge ship. He preached the gospel and passed out bread. Thousands streamed forward and made a personal commitment to Christ. I happened to meet a few of those who went forward. They told me that everyone responded in like manner because they wanted food. And the evangelist could claim something that "worked."

Service evangelism does not "count coup" every time a person responds affirmatively. Service evangelism leaves the results to God. A person might feel a yearning to "go home" and might locate the church of his or her childhood. If an encounter with a Christian encourages that, it has been effective. But only the Spirit of God knows, and only God gets the credit.

Service evangelism offers an opportunity for fellowship and team building. As our congregation has made service evangelism projects available, they have attracted a wide range of participants—everyone from old-timers (in a new church like ours, that means people who have been around for longer than two years!) to newcomers. When people come together for service, they begin to bond with each other. Those bonds affect church and interpersonal dynamics in ways that we may never fully appreciate.

I once worked on a roof-replacement project with a teenager, a recent newcomer to church, a woman who owned a business and several carpenters. In the free flow of dialogue that occured as we laid row after row of shingles, some wonderful things happened. Christians were affirmed and appreciated. People took time to listen to each other. And we expressed joy and caring in the healthiest environment possible. The church grows stronger as its people serve together.

Service evangelism roots the identity of the church (and the small group) in acts of kindness and caring. John 3:16 says, "God so loved the world that he gave . . ." First John 4:10 says, "This is love: not that we loved God, but that he loved us and sent his Son as an atoning sacrifice for our sins." Christian giving is rooted not in our ability to give anything worthwhile but in God's great gifts to the church.

When we freely give, we are acting like God. And when we act like God, we open our lives and the life of our church to the free flow of God's grace. Take two churches: a selfish church that is racked by infighting and a generous church that is always giving. Which would you rather attend? The values promoted by service evangelism tend to seep into the church, and the church inevitably becomes more caring.

Service evangelism mimics the benefits of short-term mission experiences. Many Christians pay thousands of dollars for the privilege of engaging in short-term mission and reaping its life-changing benefits. I have had such opportunities myself. Service evangelism provides similar benefits while being more accessible to people.

When we gather our mission teams together at the end of a trip for team processing, I have discovered that for many the greatest benefits were participating in service activities as part of a close-knit team. We always give the same challenge on the last evening of a mission project: "Now, take what you have learned and use it in your own hometown!" Service evangelism allows groups to continue practicing what they have learned on the mission field.

How Do You Decide What Projects to Do?

After you decide to do service evangelism, you must decide what project to do. The possibilities are limitless.

When our congregation was considering service evangelism, I found an anonymous note under my door that listed a host of options. The list included a concrete way of expressing Christian love at the local prison. Since no child care is offered to prison visitors, the person suggested that we set something up in the prison lobby to meet such a need.

Sample Service Projects

1. Simple projects
   free car wash
   grocery carrying
   snow removal
   bathroom and house cleaning
   baby clothes giveaway
   street/town/highway trash removal
   soda/candy giveaway at Little League game
2. Complex projects
   oil change/car service
   free booth (crafts/food) at county fair
   collections for pregnant teens or shut-ins (scavenger hunt?)

Planning Checklist for Projects

1. Planning
   choose from options
   obtain approvals from local congregation
   delegate logistic, groundwork and project roles
2. Logistics
   supplies
   financing/purchasing
   schedule
   safety/insurance issues
3. Groundwork
   scout site(s)
   assign project roles
4. Project
   opening assignments/prayer time/instructions
   observing how project is going/fine tuning
   conducting evaluation/sharing/prayer at end
5. Report to small group/congregation

Groups just starting service evangelism may begin with simple, nonthreatening projects such as leaf raking. Other than big dogs and gun-wielding homeowners, participants should encounter few dangers.

A brainstorming session is a good way to generate project options. Brainstorming focuses each group member on his or her participation in the community. For example, a parent with children in Little League might suggest offering free drinks at games. Or an older group member might remind the group that Tuesday is senior citizen day at the shopping market—and that carrying groceries might be a great group project.

What Issues Should We Consider in Planning a Service Evangelism Project?

How often? It is my belief that every small group, from its beginning, needs to participate in at least two service events per year. Four is even better!

It is important to bear in mind that not all methods are good for all groups. The end-of-chapter questions in the appendix are meant to help groups decide which kind of group evangelism to use.

Service evangelism provides so many positive benefits that everyone—from baby Christians to mature Christians, from starter groups to study groups—can benefit from it. To begin, you might consider planning one event and doing it well, with the intent of offering another event six months later.

What approvals do we need to obtain from our congregation? What information do we need to provide? Next you need to check with church leadership and staff to get necessary approval, and to provide publicity if you are opening your event to people outside of your group.

Getting approval from your congregation is important for two reasons. First, there are accountability issues in a group's relationship to the church. Your purpose is to feed the church and make it stronger. Communicating with church leadership is key to such a relationship. Second, there are liability and insurance issues involved in every church activity. The church is liable for any personal injuries or property damage that may occur on the project, unless it claims the project was not a church event—in which case the individuals are liable. You want your church-related activities to be noted in the records of the church so that if anything happens, you will be protected by the church and by its insurance.

What activity is likely to involve most (if not all) of our group? All projects may be helpful, but not all will be beneficial to your group. For example, a window washing event at the local grocery store might exclude participation by a handicapped group member. You need to take schedules, abilities, energy levels and desires into account during the decision-making process. Not participating in an event can make a person feel left out.

What logistics need to be covered? If you have ever participated in a poorly run event, you will understand the importance of doing your homework. Imagine showing up for a Saturday window-washing event at a local grocery store. As you arrive, you realize that nobody thought about window-washing equipment. That event may never get off the ground!

There are many logistics to consider. What equipment will we use? How will we pay any expenses that we incur? (Don't allow yourself to assume that the event planner will be happy to pay for everything.) Who will check into and obtain any necessary approvals? Who will set up?

Nobody wants to participate in a poorly outfitted project. However, you can take comfort in the fact that what you learn from earlier events can be carried over into later events. A healthy follow-up meeting, preferably the next time the group meets, should provide answers to the question, What could we do better next time?

What safety and propriety issues should we address? No group wants its service evangelism to be counterproductive. Injuries, hurt feelings and inappropriate ministry attempts will all hinder your witness.

Because there are any number of issues to address involving safety and propriety, it is difficult to summarize the kinds of questions you might consider. For example, doing an activity at a mall poses problems that are different from the ones that might be posed by raking leaves in a neighborhood.

Safety considerations involve protecting the service evangelists, the people they are serving and anyone who is in the immediate area, so that the maximum good can be accomplished. To ensure an appropriate event, consider the needs, sensitivities and insecurities of service evangelists, the people they are serving and anyone else in the immediate area.

What schedule should we keep so that our time is used most effectively? Obviously, the most time will go to the actual service event. But you may also consider planning a brief group time both before and after the event for prayer, briefing and debriefing, and sharing.

One Step Further

A group of men decided to offer a free oil change to single mothers in our area. They advertised their project through posters and newspaper announcements.

They planned the event well. They created signs to put on our church road. They created several work bays in our church parking lot. They figured out how to dispose of used oil. They had one of the volunteers agree to be a "runner" to the local car parts center for oil filters. They purchased enough oil to service many cars.

The event did not go quite as planned. Only one woman responded to the ads and posters, and nobody drove up for a free oil change. Many people slowed down and looked but appeared hesitant to accept something for nothing.

Then one member suggested changing the sign at the end of the road, inviting anyone who wanted a free oil change to drive in. Several people responded, including a husband and wife. Their oil was changed and they went on their way.

The next morning, the husband and wife returned to worship with our congregation. During the congregational sharing time, the man stood and thanked the congregation for the oil change. He said that his family was busy and under tremendous stress and appreciated the gesture.

After worship, the man revealed the source of the family's stress— their eleven-year-old son was dying. During the months that followed, congregation members helped by cleaning the house and babysitting the kids. Many prayers were offered up. In small, service-oriented ways, the church and its groups responded to a need.

As Christians obey Jesus' command to give water to the thirsty, they cannot know what extended impact their gesture may produce. But God does!

10

Groups That Care Holistically

Maxine's small group had been performing service evangelism projects for several years. Members raked leaves for widows, rotated tires for elderly friends, winterized the home of a financially strapped and jobless family, and carried groceries at the local supermarket. They had met many wonderful people and had shared God's love in a nonthreatening manner.

One evening as group members were planning their next service project, Maxine blurted out, "Don't you think there is something more we can do? I mean, service evangelism is great, and we are meeting needs, but I feel the need to care even more deeply. Does anyone else feel that same need?"

Nobody shared Maxine's concern, actually, but the idea intrigued the group, and members decided to think about it.

For the next meeting, each group member agreed to sift through newspaper and magazine articles, searching for societal needs that they might be able to address. They would then brainstorm needs and develop a plan.

Group members brought the following headlines to the next meeting:

AIDS Babies Dying in Local Hospitals

Unwed Mothers Finding Welfare to Work Difficult Because of Child Care Issues

Violent Crime Drops (But the Teen Population Is Much Lower As Well)

Alcoholism Rampant on College Campuses

Prisons Are Overcrowded

The group spent several weeks discussing, praying, arguing and planning. Their dialogue revealed facets of each other that they had never known. Maxine was a passionate and caring person who was determined to do *something*. John had strong opinions about helping people who did not want help. Marvin was a "tough love" person who had already been involved in an alcohol rehabilitation halfway house. Jean had experience in social work and was pessimistic about the group's ability to help.

Because members had agreed to operate according to group consensus, they kept talking and praying until they developed a plan that was satisfactory to everybody. They agreed to approach their church and the local prison about offering babysitting services to women with children who were visiting inmates on Saturdays.

By the time they implemented their plan, they had decided to offer the service at their church so that it could be intentionally faith oriented. Mothers with children were invited to sign up and then drop off their children without charge. The group, and several outside volunteers, taught Bible stories, did crafts that communicated gospel truths, sang and played with the children.

In time, other groups began to help. Tutoring, financial seminars and parenting courses were offered to adults. A support group/Bible study was held on Saturdays after visitation hours at the prison were over. A networking system enabled members to locate several jobs for people who needed them. And more.

Maxine's group had discovered holistic ministry.

What Is Holistic Ministry?

Holistic ministry is service that engages the whole person. While many services attempt to meet needs for different, unrelated parts of persons (a person may be sent to one office for welfare, to another for low-cost counseling and to yet another for supplemental food), holistic ministry attempts to either offer every service a person needs or, more realistically, walk a person through the change process by providing a support structure (community!).

An example of holistic ministry is the effort, gaining momentum in some states, to pair one welfare family with one congregation. The idea is for the congregation to marshal its resources to help the family locate jobs, learn budgeting, find housing, learn skills and more.

Another example of holistic ministry is the Big Brother/Big Sister program. In this program at-risk children are paired with influential adults who agree to spend time with them. Although a Big Brother does not live with his partner or provide all of the child's needs, he can have a profound impact through discussion, affirmation, challenge and accountability. Recent studies have shown that children with Big Brothers and Big Sisters perform better in life than at-risk kids without that support structure.

Still another example is Habitat for Humanity. A family that purchases a Habitat home agrees to invest "sweat equity" by working with the volunteers who construct the home, many of whom are dedicated Christians. Through their humble service Christian volunteers can have a profound impact on the family. In the give-and-take of the building environment, much more than a home is being constructed. Modeling, prayer, encouragement, support and more can be offered informally, as the Spirit directs.

Christians and Holistic Ministry

Go to any average American city and identify those who are trying to make a difference. Ask them what motivates them. You will discover that many are quiet Christians who, imitating the Master, got up from their place of privilege, wrapped a towel around their waist and began washing other people's feet. I have met countless believers serving (often unacknowledged) in the trenches, waging war against poverty and evil and pain and hurt even when negative events threaten to consume them.

Christian individuals, churches and parachurch ministries, responding to God's call, offer free or low-cost counseling, set up halfway houses for at-risk teens, visit prisons and nursing homes, run the local food pantry, volunteer for housing rehabilitation projects and offer a host of other services. This should not surprise us.

Christians are involved because we have experienced the love of Jesus Christ. We have known through Scripture and our own experience that "God so loved the world that he gave his one and only Son, that whoever believes in him shall not perish but have eternal life" (John 3:16).

Christians get involved in the world because we believe that God cares about what happens in the world. In Matthew 6, Jesus refers to God's concern for sparrows and little flowers, and then he tells us to "seek first his [God's] kingdom and his righteousness, and all these things will be given to you as well" (Matthew 6:33).

Christians leave their places of privilege because Jesus left his place in heaven to live among us. Philippians 2:5-8 provides the basis for Christian service:

Your attitude should be the same as that of Christ Jesus:

Who, being in very nature God,

did not consider equality with God something to be grasped,

but made himself nothing,

taking the very nature of a servant,

being made in human likeness.

And being found in appearance as a man,

he humbled himself

and became obedient to death—

even death on a cross!

Christians are interested in the world of the oppressed, the widow and the orphan because God directs our attention to their needs. James 1:27 says, "Religion that God our Father accepts as pure and faultless is this: to look after orphans and widows in their distress and to keep oneself from being polluted by the world." First John 3:16-17 asserts that we operate in God's love when we lay down our lives for one another and have compassion on those who are in need. "If anyone has material possessions and sees his brother in need but has no pity on him, how can the love of God be in him?" (v. 17).

Where Do We Begin?

So how should a small group respond holistically to the moral, physical and emotional decay of our society? What are the best ways to use small group resources to make a difference in the world?

There are thousands of ways for individuals in groups to get involved, and a somewhat limited number of opportunities for individual groups. Choosing one is a matter that must be prayed about, studied thoroughly and planned well. Your group's response to Christ's call for a holistic ministry can take the following steps.

Step 1: Affirm each individual's ministry in the world. Every small group member is a minister of Jesus Christ. We are his hands, his feet and his voice. Far too many Christians hide their lamp under a bushel or bury their one talent in a field. As if we could get away with being absentee servants! In reality we must minister in our communities and indeed in our world.

Our ministry can be felt in many ways. We may be the one person at work who is genuine and caring (perhaps in an unsafe work environment). We may be one of the few Little League coaches who give up notions of macho competition for affirmation, involvement and individual care. We may be the one patron frequenting the same restaurant who is positive, relaxed and considerate. Christians may exhibit a positive witness at work, at the gas pump, in the concert hall, on the airplane and in their neighborhood.

So how can we encourage one another's ministries in the world? By praying for one another! There is a subtle but profound difference between complaining about a work situation and facing that work situation as a minister of change. Responding to difficult situations with the question "What might God be calling us to do in this situation?"

opens the door to ministry.

We can also share together in prayer for those we are touching. Perhaps a volunteer who works with the high-school band has met a troubled student. The student has poured out his heart, sharing deep hurt and pain. The small group member then comes to the group with a request for prayer, as well as an openness to receive feedback and advice on how to proceed. The group in those moments can pray for the member and the teen and can provide an accountability for the mentor as she acts in ministry.

Step 2: Study the issues. At some point, every group should consider societal issues by studying resources together. As I write this chapter, a profound debate about assisted suicide is taking place in America. I am aware from my reading on this subject that simplistic knee-jerk arguments are being put forth by both sides in the debate.

If assisted suicide becomes a legal option to Americans, what implications should Christians consider? What might caring Christians do to prepare for involvement in life-and-death decisions? What might caring Christians do to offer a safe place for those who might become unwanted (and unaffordable) in future society? What education and information can Christians provide those who care for the elderly, infirm or mentally impaired?

There are many such issues that bear serious study. Changes in welfare benefits are going to affect society as a whole. Groups may benefit from reading a book like *Resurrecting Hope: Powerful Stories of How God Is Moving to Reach Our Cities,* by John Perkins. Groups interested in the political arena might find Tony Campolo's *Is Jesus a Republican or a Democrat? and Fourteen Other Polarizing Issues* provocative. And groups interested in discussing larger issues related to the church's involvement in the world could read St. Augustine's *City of God,* or *Resident Aliens* by Will Willimon and Stanley Hauerwas.

Step 3: Discuss an incarnational approach to group ministry. Incarnational ministry is a "ministry of presence." Groups that decide to serve in this way are determined to make themselves available to people on a significant level.

Go to the hardware store in your town, pick up a Wet Paint sign and tape it to the wall of a hallway somewhere. Then retreat to a corner with a camcorder and record the results. As you may guess, many people, especially those who somehow think they are not being observed, will surreptitiously touch the wall.

There is something riveting about being told no. It makes us want to look into the matter. Adam and Eve were not successful at navigating the tension between obedience and disobedience. They were great, however, at passing on rebellious genes to their offspring. Those who are involved in the ministry of helping people holistically need to give up pointing fingers and sermonizing about the sin that got them in trouble in the first place.

God's final response to our rebellion was not a lecture. Nor was it a severe reprimand or an imposing judgment. Instead, it was Jesus' incarnation.

In its own way, the incarnation was a lecture. But Jesus had a way of speaking that drew people to him. The incarnation was also a reprimand because Jesus is so different from all that we know. It was also judgment because Jesus had to die—but he died in our place so that we could escape the judgment. The incarnation was all of these, but so much more. "The Word became flesh and tabernacled among us," according to John 1 (literal translation). We might say that God came alongside us, touching us at our point of need in order to call us to a place specially designed for us.

Incarnational ministry presents a challenge. It is easy to sit and debate the effectiveness of time limits on welfare or whether certain people deserve help or not. You don't incur much risk when you lash out at transvestites and adulterers, pigeonholing them in the locations that you deem worthy of them.

It is more difficult to care by coming alongside a person. Yet people are more likely to change when a caring person works with them instead of remaining far removed from their problems. Lawmakers can have some impact on people's problems, but it is usually from a distance. Caring Christians have the ultimate impact because they get close enough to bring change. Groups employing incarnational ministry may want to consider the following three issues: (1) the difference between helping and empowering, (2) understanding and defining boundaries, and (3) allowing people to make their own choices.

First, know the difference between helping and empowering. There are always issues of power involved when one person attempts to help another. The helper comes from a position of power. It can feel good to help. Many people volunteer for nonthreatening helping opportunities precisely because they enjoy the feeling that accompanies making a difference.

But helping is not always empowering. I once worked in a soup kitchen with a group of well-meaning friends from my church. They enjoyed rolling up their sleeves and producing wonderful meals. People would come shuffling in and sit down to a wonderful variety of home-cooked meals. But the cooks and the diners rarely interacted. Whenever I put myself in the place of those being served, I knew that I would have felt helpless and unable to choose. How to reverse such dynamics?

Why not invite some of the volunteers to sit with the guests? They could develop ongoing relationships, and their conversation could provide genuine opportunities for people (both helpers and guests) to make a change in their lives. Helping can be fun; empowering is much better. Empowering begins when you start listening and caring, taking time out of serving to value those you are working with.

Second, understand and define your boundaries. Caring persons need to avoid becoming entangled in emotion-sapping relationships that can threaten their time with family, their relaxation and even their sleep. The way around such dynamics is to define healthy boundaries on your involvement in people's lives.

We describe our boundaries every time we are around others. Someone who freely uses the words *I love you* and touches frequently has wide boundaries. Another person communicates narrow boundaries through spare language and touch. The healthiest boundaries fall somewhere in the middle and leave a person free enough to encourage interaction but honest enough to insist on a reasonable amount of personal space.

Third, allow people to make and live with their own choices. Persons living in Western cultures have experienced many positive benefits from living in progressive countries. Most have at least some access to schooling, medicine and personal opportunity. Those who miss out on such benefits can feel victimized.

Some people make bad choices and apparently have no desire to change. Anyone who wants to help others will at some point confront such a person. So how can we keep such a person from repeating destructive cycles, usually while putting the blame on others or on the system?

Require some choices from people—no matter how small. I have a friend who runs an inner-city ministry that brings in homeless women, equips them with skills, finds them jobs, and eventually moves them and their families on. One day we were walking through one of the ministry's apartment buildings when my friend saw a woman still dressed in her pajamas in the middle of the day. After a somewhat animated conversation, that woman was dressed and ready for work. I would almost be willing to bet that she did not make that mistake again.

Helping people (sometimes requiring them) to make choices actually empowers them to gain control of themselves. They are to choose where they work. They are to follow through. They are to keep their living area clean. They are to stop verbally and physically abusing another person. And all of these choices carry consequences, for better or worse.

Step 4: Brainstorm ideas. There are several avenues of ministry to consider as you brainstorm. First, the group may minister to an individual; for example, it may "adopt" a pregnant teen and walk her through pregnancy, childbirth and motherhood or adoption. Or it may work with an at-risk teen (among other alternatives).

Second, the group may minister to a family; for example, it may sponsor a refugee family or a family attempting to leave the welfare system (among other alternatives).

Third, the group may minister to a group; for example, it may serve regularly at a soup kitchen, a nursing home or some other human service location, developing long-term relationships that may blossom into opportunities to genuinely help someone.

Step 5: Perform further research, get approvals and implement the ministry. Because helping people involves such complex factors as human motivation, personal circumstances and many other variables, you will want to give careful consideration to as many perspectives as possible while you are designing the ministry. The best way to design a helping ministry is to identify an organization that you believe is doing it right. Interview people from such an organization and allow them to critique your ideas so that you can draw on their wisdom as much as possible.

When Christians Care

A number of years ago I was walking along a road when I saw a young man with a pronounced limp moving in the opposite direction. God touched my heart, so I moved toward him and began conversing with him. I discovered that he had been involved in a car accident as a child that left him physically and mentally impaired for life.

I cultivated a friendship with this young man that lasted for a few years, until I moved. We would meet regularly, perhaps every other week, over games of chess, local basketball games or conversations on his front porch. My compassion was stirred when I discovered that local children tormented him. They would knock him over, tease him and make allegations of sexual harassment (which would have been impossible in his case).

As I look back on that situation, I am amazed that he trusted me. If I were harassed and tormented in like manner, I would probably become bitter. But he basked in the warmth of our relationship, always positive and eager to please. He invited Jesus into his life, and God used me to bring a small ray of holistic healing to his life.

When we Christians care, we are acting as Jesus would act in the same situations. When we Christians care, we are offering the light of hope to a world of pessimism and darkness. When we Christians care, we put our light on a hill where it draws attention to God.

Sample Holistic Missions

1. Tutoring at-risk teens and children
2. Tutoring GED students
3. Sponsoring a welfare family coming off the rolls or acting as a personal advocate for welfare and social security recipients
4. Offering seminars and/or counseling in financial and life skills

Appendix 1

Questions for
Reflection & Discussion

This section contains questions that will enhance both individual and group experience when interacting with *Small Group Outreach: Turning Groups Inside Out*. Questions for individuals fall under the heading "Reflection on the Chapter" for each chapter in the book. Questions for groups fall under the heading "Small Group Discussion" for each chapter of the book.

The optimal way to learn from this book is to participate in a small group that agrees to study this book together. Individuals may read the assigned chapter and then carefully answer the "Reflection on the Chapter" questions for that chapter. Afterward, you may process what you are learning by using the "Small Group Discussion" outline.

Space does not permit a discussion of healthy small-group principles. Appendix 2 contains a helpful and thorough small group covenant. By using or adapting this covenant and following through on it, you will better ensure a positive group experience.

Chapter 1: Becoming a SAFE Group
Reflection on the Chapter

1. When, in your experience, have you ever witnessed a similar story to the one at the beginning of the chapter (about the workers in the plant whose friend died)?

2. What are some ways that groups can turn people off to Jesus Christ?

3. Describe in your own words what a SAFE group is.

4. How would you describe each of the dimensions of a SAFE group?

☐ Sharing personal stories

☐ Articulating faith

☐ Fostering dynamic ministry

☐ Engendering intragroup caring

5. Which of the dimensions of a SAFE group does the group you participate in do well?

6. Which of the dimensions of a SAFE group does the group you participate in not do well?

Small Group Discussion

1. Discuss questions 1 and 2 above.

2. This chapter contains an illustration about a smelly car salesman. What is an instance when you have been turned off by a difficult salesperson?

How did you respond to the salesperson?

3. The book of Ephesians provides a fascinating glimpse into what it means to be part of God's kingdom. Contained in the first two chapters are three "moving picture" glimpses of what it means to be a child of God (Ephesians 1:3-14; 2:1-10, 11-22). The moving picture located in Ephesians 2:11-22 offers the best glimpse of a SAFE group. Read Ephesians 2:11-22.

4. What is the "story" that is hinted at in this passage?

5. Locate each of these "stages" of spirituality in the passage.

☐ Complete exclusion from God

☐ Involvement with Jesus Christ

☐ Involvement with one another

☐ Unified participation in God's kingdom building

☐ Filled (together) with the Spirit of God

Is this kind of activity and movement happening in your congregation? Why or why not?

Is this kind of activity and movement happening in your small group? Why or why not?

6. Reading just a little bit into the text, see if you can locate the

elements of a SAFE group in this passage.

☐ Sharing personal stories (of God's work in our lives)

☐ Articulating faith together (exploring the dimensions of God's mercy and grace)

☐ Fostering dynamic ministry

☐ Engendering intragroup caring

7. Which of the four elements of a SAFE group does your group currently possess?

8. Which does your group need to work on?

9. Of the practical suggestions located in the chapter (and some you develop yourselves), which can you work to develop as a group?

10. Pray that God will help you become a SAFE group.

Chapter 2: Developing an Out-Reaching Vision
Reflection on the Chapter

1. According to the chapter, what are things that small groups do well?

2. What are some of the weaknesses of the small group movement?

3. Intention to do outreach is not enough. Groups and individuals who want to share their faith need to also address six potential problems. In your own words, describe each problem.

☐ Cozy Group

☐ Heady Group

☐ Haphazard Group

☐ Static Group

☐ Dysfunctional Group

☐ Self-Centered Group

4. Which of the six potential problems do you believe is or might be a weakness in the small group you participate in?

What can the group do to address the problem(s)?

Small Group Discussion

1. Discuss questions 1 and 2 above.

2. Describe a person you know with an obnoxious Christian witness (don't name names!).

3. How do you respond to the person?

4. In the Old Testament there are numerous references to the purpose of the temple, which was to be the earthly location where God's "Name" resided. The temple was to serve as a place of reconciliation (sacrifice), worship and outreach (as all nations saw God's love for Israel and began to seek his face as well). Instead, the Israelites hoarded God's blessings and their witness was muted. Read Mark 11:12-19.

5. How is the barren fig tree like the nation of Israel throughout its history?

6. In this chapter of the book, six different group witness problems were identified (see question 3 above). According to Mark 11, which (there may be more than one) of these problems did the Jewish church possess?

7. In verse 17 Jesus offers God's vision for the temple. In your own words, what is that vision?

8. What is your vision for the impact your group can have on the church and world?

9. Which of the six group problems might be an issue for your group? What can you do to address each of the group problems you have?

10. Bring your vision and group problems before God. As you pray, you may choose to stand in a circle holding hands, allowing people to offer brief prayers as they are comfortable.

Chapter 3: Groups That Invite

Reflection on the Chapter

1. How do you respond to the story (about the author's Continental Singers evangelism experience) at the beginning of this chapter, and why?

☐ I understand completely.

☐ You should have had more faith that everything would work out.

☐ I want to care, but just don't always know how.

☐ I could never have sat down with the young man and led him to Christ.

2. What is "strength in numbers" evangelism?

"side door" evangelism?

"high risk/high grace" evangelism?

3. "Prayer is not just helpful in changing the heart of the person prayed for; God also changes the heart of the pray-er." Explain what this means.

4. Who have you talked about your group experience(s) with?

If you have not shared your group experience(s) with anybody, who can you tell?

5. How can telling people about small group experiences help in witnessing?

6. Which of the group evangelism options discussed in this chapter do you feel is most suited to your group?

7. Who are persons in your natural network (family, friends, work associates, neighbors) that you believe might benefit from small group evangelism?

Small Group Discussion

1. Discuss questions 1 and 2 above.

2. What fears get attached to the words *evangelism, outreach* and *witness?*

3. Why do you think Christians are scared to share their faith more openly?

4. If you have shared Jesus with another person, offer a brief synopsis of what you encountered and how you felt.

5. Acts 12 involves an interesting story about Peter being released from prison because of the prayers of the faith community. While Acts 12 does not specifically address witnessing issues, it closes with these words: "But the Word of God continued to increase and spread." Read Acts 12:1-17, 24.

6. Describe the events that take place in this passage.

7. Why is the element of disbelief (Peter thought he was dreaming, and the believers did not believe Rhoda the maid) so prominent in this story?

8. What does this passage teach us about who is really in charge of the world?

about the power of prayer?

about absolute dependence on God?

about the methods God will use to spread the good news?

9. Discuss some of the steps described in this chapter of the book (answer only those that apply to your situation).

☐ Who will we pray for?

☐ How can we prepare ourselves to be more effective witnesses?

☐ What strengths of our group are worth telling others about?

☐ Which option best fits our situation: invite people all year, invite people during a special time in the year, use either support, recovery or "Jesus" material?

☐ How conducive is our location to effective witness?

☐ How conducive is our room setup (including noise and distractions) for witness?

☐ How might we adjust our schedule to more effectively share our faith with a newcomer?

☐ What should we do about our homework demands to foster more effective witness?

10. After reading the first three chapters, how do you feel about small group evangelism?

11. Pray that God will direct your group to the kind of issues and evangelistic method he has chosen. Name specific concerns that have been raised in your time together.

Chapter 4: Groups That Multiply
Reflection on the Chapter

1. What, in your estimation, were some of the problems in Marjorie's group?

2. Why does growth often produce a crisis?

3. Why is stagation a form of group death?

4. Consider the following ideas from the chapter:

☐ What are key issues in inviting and assimilating newcomers?

☐ What is the cell small group concept?

☐ What is the meta small group concept?

☐ What does it mean to be an open group? closed group? open/closed group?

☐ Why use an empty chair at meetings?

☐ Why use groups of four for sharing and prayer, for groups larger than seven?

5. How are apprentice leaders helpful?

How do you train apprentice leaders?

6. Describe the process of birthing groups according to the following models:

☐ Mother-daughter

☐ Reverse split

☐ Apprentice begins new group

☐ Leader begins new group

☐ Incubation

☐ Turbo group

7. Why should groups go through a closure process when they end?

8. Describe the following termination strategies:

☐ crockpot ☐ oven bake ☐ microwave

9. Why, in your opinion, aren't there more "third-generation" (which means that one group has birthed a second group, which in turn has birthed another) groups?

Small Group Discussion

1. Discuss questions 1 through 3. What details do you know about your birth?

2. What details can you share from the birth of any children, nieces or nephews?

3. How do you feel about the possibility of your group's birthing another group(s) as God blesses it?

☐ Let's do it!

☐ I think it sounds great, but I would rather keep this group together.

☐ I think it sounds great, but I don't think we're ready yet.

☐ I don't understand why someone would want to break up this group.

☐ Other

4. Read Acts 8:1-8.

5. How is the persecution described in Acts 8:1 a fulfillment of Jesus' words in Acts 1:8?

6. Saul's moving from "house to house" suggests that the early church was in reality a small group movement. What did Saul (eventually renamed Paul) do to the believing community?

7. According to Acts 8:4 what was the response of the believers to their scattering?

8. According to Acts 8:8, what was the source of joy for the believers?

9. In what ways is the scattering in Acts 8 similar to the dynamics involved in a multiplying small group movement?

In what ways is it different?

10. Discuss how the following group design issues might be helpful to your group:

☐ open group, closed group or open/closed group

☐ the "empty chair" discipline

☐ sharing and prayer in groups of four

☐ apprenticing leaders

11. What are group strengths that will help us to grow and multiply?

12. What are group concerns that will inhibit our growth and multiplication?

13. What should we do to prepare for multiplication?

14. Allow time for prayer.

Chapter 5: Groups That Serve the Church

Reflection on the Chapter

1. According to the example at the beginning of the chapter, what were positive ways that Chuck's group impacted his congregation?

2. What are ways that churches may unknowingly create nonrelational environments that stifle creativity and spiritual life?

3. Explain the significance of Jesus' key pronouncements:

☐ the Great Commandment   ☐ the New Commandment

☐ the Great Prayer   ☐ the Great Commission

4. What are the shortcomings of cliques?

5. How might a "koinonia-based clique" allow a small group to positivley influence its congregation?

6. What are the two temptations of small groups in relation to serving

their congregation?

7. What are some positive ministries your group could do within your congregation?

8. Why, in most cases, would it be most helpful for the small group to confess and surrender rather than withdrawing and leaving?

9. Interview several people each from the following groups, asking them what they feel the strengths of your church are, what its weaknesses are and why people might either not come or end up leaving the church: church insiders, people on the fringe of the church, people who have left the church, people who don't go to church but are familiar with your church.

Small Group Discussion

1. Allow each person to answer questions 1 and 2 above.

2. What is a favorite restaurant to you?

3. What of the following makes you like the restaurant (name all that apply)? ☐ mood (decoration, architecture) ☐ atmosphere ☐ service ☐ familiarity ☐ hors d'oeuvres ☐ food ☐ drinks ☐ dessert ☐ other

4. Just as restaurants involve much more than food, so churches involve much more than teaching. Examine the following list and grade your congregation (with 1 being bad and 5 being superior):

___ architecture

___ accessibility (location, handicapped)

___ friendliness

___ familiarity (ability to locate places, to find seats)

___ genuineness of worship

___ focus on the "little things" (keeping up with people, following up visitors)

5. Read Matthew 5:13-16.

6. Your small group is to be "salt." What does salt do?

7. Why is our "taste" important as a testimony of God's grace in our lives?

8. How is your small group either effective or ineffective in being salt to the church?

9. Your small group is to be "light." What does light do?

10. Where salt is subtle, light is dramatic. What does being "light" to

the congregation have to do with people seeing our "good works"?

11. How is your small group either effective or ineffective in doing good works in the church?

12. The chapter argues that our small groups are an extension of the church. Discuss your church's weaknesses. How might they be manifest in the lives and ministry of your small group?

How might the surrender and group-focus prayers discussed in the chapter be helpful to you?

13. What ministry might God be calling us to, as we try to be light to our church?

14. Ask God to guide you as you seek to be faithful to his leading in the building up of the body of Christ.

Chapter 6: Groups That Support Mission
Reflection on the Chapter

1. Mission heroes provide positive examples of important Christian virtues. What are some of these virtues?

2. What is a significant weakness of the "lone ranger" style of mission work?

3. Why must the church be the "base camp" for missionaries?

4. What were the significant differences between the churches in the two scenarios presented in the chapter (Christ the King Church and First Church)?

5. Explain what mission involvement in each of these areas might include for a group: ☐ prayer support ☐ concrete expressions of friendship ☐ supporting a mission family ☐ supporting a missionary child ☐ going

6. Of the ideas presented, which do you feel your group will *not* be able to accomplish? Why?

7. Of the ideas presented, which do you feel your group will be able to accomplish? Why?

Small Group Discussion

1. Allow each person to answer questions 1 through 3 above.

2. When you were growing up, who was one of your heroes? Why?

3. Who is a church/Christian hero for you (local, national, international, past or present)?

4. How effective is your church's involvement in mission?

5. Read Luke 24:44-53.

6. This is Luke's version of Christ's commission to his discipes. When did these events occur (see also vv. 36-43)?

7. Why did Christ's "opening their minds" accompany their call to mission?

8. How could Christ's opening *our* minds accompany our call to mission?

9. Look again at verses 47-48. What is repentance?

What is involved in proclaiming forgiveness of sins?

How does the church model God's forgiveness of sins in the world?

10. Notice, we are not told to "witness to" these things, but that we are witness *of* these things. This implies that, far from being in control, we will see God's mighty hand at work. What are ways that the disciples witnessed God's work in and through them?

11. Based on this commission, what is every Christian's call to mission and responsibility in mission?

12. Of the five ideas presented in this chapter, which do you think your group might be capable of doing at this time?

Consider assigning several of the possibilites to group members for research and a presentation at a later group meeting.

13. Ask God to guide you as you seek to be faithful to his leading in mission involvement.

Chapter 7: Groups That Go on Short-Term Mission
Reflection on the Chapter

1. Why did Sharon's group hesitate when she mentioned short-term mission (in the illustration at the beginning of this chapter)?

2. What might make you hesitate before participating in a short-term project?

3. Explain the benefits of short-term mission:

☐ risk

☐ community
☐ interaction
☐ long-term change

   4. Why might short-term missionaries romanticize the people they are serving?

   5. What is the danger of romanticizing the people you are serving?

   6. What kinds of things should a short-term mission group do to prepare?

   7. Explain the significance of flexibility in maximizing the project. What is the role of group process?

   8. What are some of the potential outcomes of short-term mission?

Small Group Discussion

   1. Allow each person to answer questions 1 through 3 above.

   2. Have you ever participated in a service or short-term mission project? If so, what was it like? If not, what struck you most about the mission projects described?

   3. After reading this chapter, how do you feel about short-term mission?

☐ Ready to go! ☐ Maybe I'll try it someday. ☐ I'm not sure it's for me.
☐ I'm not sure I could do it. ☐ It's not for me!

   4. Read Mark 6:6b-13.

   5. Jesus sent his disciples out on a short-term mission trip. What kind of "team-building" occurred before he sent them? (See the earlier chapters of Mark for ideas.)

   6. Jesus had considered all of the logistics necessary for this trip to be a success. What were the details of his instructions given in this passage?

   7. Why might Jesus have sent them in pairs?

   told them to carry no bread, bag, money and so on?

   told them to shake the dust off of their feet if his message was rejected?

   8. How must the disciples have felt at "their" ability to do Jesus' ministry: preach, cast out demons and heal the sick?

   9. What can we learn about short-term mission from this passage?

10. How do you feel about the possibility of a short-term mission project? (Each person can answer.)

11. If we were to go, where might we go, and what might we do?

Consider assigning several of the possibilites to group members for research and a presentation at a later group meeting.

12. Ask God to guide you as you seek to be faithful to his leading in short-term mission involvement.

Chapter 8: Groups That Evangelize

Reflection on the Chapter

1. What is your initial response to the illustration at the beginning of the chapter?

☐ I feel sorry for those groups that didn't do so well.

☐ Why did they break up such a good thing?

☐ I'm excited about the risks they took.

2. How does small group evangelism represent the "attack subtly from within" strategy?

How does evangelistic small group ministry represent the "attack from the border" strategy?

3. What are the benefits of evangelistic small groups?

4. What are the potential downfalls and difficulties of evangelistic small groups?

5. How would you describe "preevangelistic" small groups?

6. What are examples of such groups?

7. How would you describe evangelistic small groups?

8. How would you describe cross-cultural small groups?

9. Of the three kinds of evangelistic groups mentioned in this chapter, which appeals to you most? Why?

Which is most difficult for you to envision yourself doing? Why?

Small Group Discussion

1. Answer questions 1 and 2 above.

2. What are you like when you talk about something important?

☐ I can be too pushy.

☐ I'm too laid back.

☐ I sometimes get carried away.

☐ I think people like hearing me talk about something that is important to me.

3. What is your risk-taking level?

☐ I love big risks.

☐ I hate risk.

☐ Some risk I can handle, most I can't.

☐ Most risk I can handle, some I can't.

4. Read Matthew 25:14-30.

5. Recap in your own words what happens in this story.

6. What are Christians who read this passage challenged to do with our talents?

7. The focus of the context is that we must live in a state of preparedness for the return of the Master (Jesus Christ). It is not unthinkable in the context to supply the phrase "opportunities for evangelism" where we see the word *talent*. A talent is a gift (like salvation); it is meant to be invested (like evangelism); it bears fruit as we learn to risk (in the salvation of others). If evangelism is equivalent to a talent, is your group a one-talent, two-talent or five-talent group (in its potential for evangelism)?

What kinds of things might God challenge you to invest in so that you get a return for God's investment?

8. Discuss the three types of evangelistic groups listed in this chapter. Which best suits your group?

9. Of all the ideas presented in chapters of the book so far, which do you feel strongest about?

10. Ask God to direct your group to the kind of issues and evangelistic method he has chosen. Name specific concerns that have been raised in your time together.

Chapter 9: Groups That Serve the Community

Reflection on the Chapter

1. What is service evangelism?

2. What are examples of service evangelism?

3. The chapter explains that service evangelism is great evangelism training. Why do you think many Christians feel guilty about evangelism?

What are positive ways that service evangelism might equip people to more effectively share their faith with others?

4. Explain each of the benefits of service evangelism.

☐ allows Christians to witness to non-Christians

☐ offers opportunity for fellowship and team building

☐ creates a church culture of love and sharing

☐ mimics the benefits of short-term mission trips

5. What do you believe to be potential service evangelism projects your group might participate in?

6. What are potential hindrances to your group's performing service evangelism?

7. In the closing section, "One Step Further," a story was told about a family responding to a free oil change. How did you feel when reading the story?

Why is it important for a church to be prepared to follow through on relationships begun on a service project?

Small Group Discussion

1. Allow each person to answer questions one through three.

2. Tell about a time in your life that somebody has done an act of kindness for you.

3. What is your natural reaction when you receive acts of unsolicited kindness?

4. How effective do you believe your church and small group are at showing Christian love (with no strings attached)?

☐ We care deeply and show it.

☐ We care deeply and don't often show it.

☐ We care somewhat but don't go out of our way for others.

☐ We don't seem to care and rarely show it.

☐ We don't care.

5. Read Matthew 25:31-46.

6. What kinds of activities did the "sheep" engage in?

7. What kinds of people did they meet?

8. Who did the sheep really meet when they helped someone (v. 40)?

9. From this parable, what quality is part of all God's children?

10. Discuss service evangelism. What excites you about it? What are your questions and concerns?

11. For practice (or for real!) plan a service evangelism project.

☐ Choose the project.

☐ Discuss how to include/involve your local congregation in planning and implementation.

☐ Choose a time and a place for the project.

☐ Discuss logistics like materials and safety issues.

☐ Devise a project schedule that includes briefing before and debriefing afterward.

12. Pray that God will guide you as you seek to be faithful to his leading in the building up of the body of Christ.

Chapter 10: Groups That Care Holistically

Reflection on the Chapter

1. Examine the process employed by Maxine's group to discover their call to holistic ministry. What were its strengths?

What might you have added to the process?

2. What is holistic ministry?

3. What are positive examples of holistic ministry that you know about?

4. Why do you think Christians are often at the forefront of efforts to help others?

5. If you had to choose a potential holistic ministry for your group, what would it be for you?

6. What is an issue(s) that concerns you, that you would like to learn more about?

7. What are examples (attempt to create your own) of holistic group ministry to an individual?

a family?

a group?

8. What is the difference between helping and empowering?

9. What are boundaries that you would want to protect as you get involved in others' lives (for example, family time)?

Small Group Discussion

1. Discuss questions one through three above.

2. When is a time in life that you were in trouble and needed help? Did someone come to your rescue?

3. How have you been involved in holistic ministry?

4. Who is a person you know that is involved in holistic ministry? Describe the ministry.

5. Read Nehemiah 1:1-11.

6. What does Nehemiah 1:1-3 say about the plight of Nehemiah's people?

7. Attempt to "fill in the details." What must life have been like in Jerusalem in relation to the safety and security of people from criminals and enemies?

the prospects for work, advancement and provision?

8. What was Nehemiah's response to the news?

9. Why did Nehemiah confess *his* sins as those of his people, and their sins as his?

10. What happened as a result of Nehemiah's prayer? (If nobody in your group knows the story of Nehemiah, attempt to get a study Bible and read its introduction and outline to see what happens in the rest of the book.)

11. What is something about your culture/country that concerns you deeply, that you believe God may want you to be involved in?

12. What is an opportunity you have right now (at work, in your neighborhood, wherever) that is an opportunity for you to practice holistic ministry?

13. What are prospects your group may have for holistic ministry?

14. If there is the desire to do it, how can your group prepare to do holistic ministry?

15. Take time to pray together.

Appendix 2

Sample Small Group Covenant

Few issues are as vital to the long-term health of a group as the group covenant. A positive group covenant explains who you are and defines your goals, your structure and your expectations. It also sets forth the disciplines that you wish to employ. Groups that construct a covenant carefully and then follow it position themselves for growth. What follows is a sample covenant, which you may use and adapt as necessary (covenant adapted from *Small Group Starter Kit,* InterVarsity Press).

Part I: We reflect the wishes, needs and abilities of our members.
Length of covenant: from _____ to _____
We will study the following:
Each participant will be expected to complete the following work during the week (if any):
Meeting time_____ Place_____
Duration_____
Type of group:
Group focus/purpose:
Childcare issues:
Childcare discipline issues (how we will address behavioral problems):

Part II: We meet together.
Schedule of meeting (how much time spent for study? prayer? sharing? outreach?)

Part III: We are accountable to one another.

  We agree to the following (check those that apply):

  ___Sharing and prayer in groups of four

  ___Honesty

  ___Affirmation of one another

  ___Decision-making by group consensus

  ___No gossip

Part IV: Everyone is important to the group.

  Group roles:

  Leader _____

  Apprentice_____

  Host/hostess _____

  Prayer leader_____

  Other (fellowship leader, outreach leader, timekeeper, etc.)

Part V: We welcome newcomers.

  We are an

  ___open group

  ___open/closed group

Part VI: We are growing.

  To grow spiritually, our goals are

  To welcome newcomers, our goals are

  To grow relationally, our goals are

  To grow through outreach, our goals are

Appendix 3

Resources for Further Reading

Chapter 1: Becoming a SAFE Group

Donahue, Bill. *The Willow Creek Guide to Leading Life-Changing Small Groups*. Grand Rapids, Mich.: Zondervan, 1996.

Long, Jimmy, et al. *Small Group Leaders' Handbook: The Next Generation*. Downers Grove, Ill.: InterVarsity Press, 1995.

Chapter 2: Developing an Out-Reaching Vision

Arnold, Jeffrey. *The Big Book on Small Groups*. Downers Grove, Ill.: InterVarsity Press, 1991.

Chapter 3: Groups That Invite

Arnold, Jeffrey. *Small Group Starter Kit*. Downers Grove, Ill.: InterVarsity Press, 1994.

Coleman, Robert. *The Master Plan of Discipleship*. Grand Rapids, Mich.: Revell, 1987.

———. *The Master Plan of Evangelism*. 1963. Reprint, Grand Rapids, Mich.: Revell, 1987.

Petersen, Jim. *Living Proof: Sharing the Gospel Naturally*. Colorado Springs, Colo.: NavPress, 1990.

Chapter 4: Groups That Multiply

Cho, Paul Yonggi, and Harold Hostetler. *Successful Home Cell Groups*. Plainfield, N.J.: Logos International, 1981.

George, Carl. *The Coming Church Revolution*. Grand Rapids, Mich.: Revell, 1994.

————. *Prepare Your Church for the Future*. Grand Rapids, Mich.: Revell, 1991.

Mack, Michael, with Jeffrey Arnold. *Developing Leaders to Multiply Ministry: Training Apprentices and Coaches to Birth New Groups and Make Disciples*. Cincinnati: Small Group Network, 1996.

Neighbour, Ralph W., Jr. *Where Do We Go from Here? A Guidebook for the Cell Group Church*. Houston: Touch Publications, 1990.

Chapter 5: Groups That Serve the Church

Barna, George. *Turnaround Churches: How to Overcome Barriers to Growth and Bring New Life to an Established Church*. Ventura, Calif.: Regal, 1991.

————. *User Friendly Churches: What Christians Need to Know About the Churches People Love to Go To*. Ventura, Calif.: Regal, 1991.

Mack, Michael. *The Synergy Church: A Strategy for Integrating Small Groups and Sunday School*. Grand Rapids, Mich.: Baker Book House, 1996.

Stedman, Ray. *Body Life*. Ventura, Calif.: Regal, 1972.

Chapter 6: Groups That Support Mission

Kane, J. Herbert. *Wanted: World Christians*. Grand Rapids, Mich.: Baker Book House, 1986.

Chapter 7: Groups That Go on Short-Term Mission

Gaukroger, Stephen. *Your Mission, Should You Accept It . . .* Downers Grove, Ill.: InterVarsity Press, 1996.

Chapter 8: Groups That Evangelize

Jacks, Bob, and Betty Jacks, with Ron Wormser Sr. *Your Home, a Lighthouse: Hosting an Evangelistic Bible Study*. Colorado Springs, Colo.: NavPress, 1986.

Peace, Richard. *Small Group Evangelism: A Training Program for*

Reaching Out with the Gospel. Downers Grove, Ill.: InterVarsity Press, 1985.

Scazzero, Peter. *Introducing Jesus: Starting an Investigative Bible Study for Seekers*. Downers Grove, Ill.: InterVarsity Press, 1991.

Chapter 9: Groups That Serve the Community

Sjogren, Steve. *Conspiracy of Kindness: A Refreshing New Approach to Sharing the Love of Jesus with Others*. Ann Arbor, Mich.: Servant, 1993.

Chapter 10: Groups That Care Holistically

Campolo, Tony. *Is Jesus a Republican or a Democrat? and Fourteen Other Polarizing Issues*. Dallas: Word, 1995.

Perkins, John. *Resurrecting Hope: Powerful Stories of How God Is Moving to Reach Our Cities*. Ventura, Calif.: Regal, 1995.

Willimon, William, and Stanley Hauerwas. *Resident Aliens*. Nashville: Abingdon, 1989.

Notes

Chapter 1: Becoming a SAFE Group
[1]Win Arn and Charles Arn, *The Master's Plan* (Pasadena, Calif.: Church Growth Press, 1987), p. 43.

Chapter 2: Developing an Out-Reaching Vision
[1]Robert Wuthnow, *Sharing the Journey: Support Groups and America's New Quest for Spirituality* (New York: Free Press, 1994), pp. 45-48.
[2]Ibid., p. 25.

Chapter 3: Groups That Invite
[1]Steve Sjogren, *Conspiracy of Kindness* (Ann Arbor, Mich.: Servant, 1993), pp. 53-73.

Chapter 4: Groups That Multiply
[1]Jeffrey Arnold, *The Big Book on Small Groups* (Downers Grove, Ill.: InterVarsity Press, 1991), pp. 178-79.
[2]Ralph Neighbour, *Where Do We Go from Here? A Guidebook for the Cell Group Church* (Houston, Tex.: Touch Publications, 1990), pp. 197-208.
[3]Carl George, *Prepare Your Church for the Future* (Grand Rapids, Mich.: Revell, 1991), p. 113.

Chapter 6: Groups That Support Mission
[1]Herbert Kane, *Wanted: World Christians* (Grand Rapids, Mich.: Baker Book House, 1986), p. 19.
[2]John Kule, ed., *Perspectives on the Unfinished Task* (Ventura, Calif.: Regal, 1984), p. 89.

Chapter 8: Groups That Evangelize
[1]Bob Jacks and Betty Jacks, *Your Home, a Lighthouse: Hosting an Evangelistic Bible Study* (Colorado Springs, Colo.: NavPress, 1986), p. 29.
[2]Richard Peace, *Small Group Evangelism: A Training Program for Reaching Out with the Gospel* (Downers Grove, Ill.: InterVarsity Press, 1985), p. 13.
[3]Jacks and Jacks, *Your Home, a Lighthouse*, p. 17.
[4]Peter Scazzero, *Introducing Jesus: Starting an Investigative Bible Study for Seekers* (Downers Grove, Ill.: InterVarsity Press, 1991), p. 21.

Chapter 9: Groups That Serve the Community

[1]Rebecca Manley Pippert, *Out of the Saltshaker and into the World* (Downers Grove, Ill.: InterVarsity Press, 1979).

[2]Sjogren, *Conspiracy of Kindness,* pp. 107-8.